by Meg Merrill

NATURE IN NEEDLEPOINT
A GARDENER'S BOOK OF NEEDLEPOINT

A Gardener's

Book of Needlepoint

by
Jack Bodi
Meg Merrill
Catherine di Montezemolo

INTRODUCTION BY C. Z. GUEST

PHOTOGRAPHS BY JOE LEOMBRUNO
AND GIANNI LAMI

Simon and Schuster   New York

Published by Simon and Schuster
A Division of Gulf & Western Corporation
Simon & Schuster Building
Rockefeller Center
1230 Avenue of the Americas
New York, New York 10020

Graphs by Jill Weber
Manufactured in the United States of America

1 2 3 4 5 6 7 8 9 10

Library of Congress Cataloging in Publication Data
Bodi, Jack.
    A gardener's book of needlepoint.
    Bibliography: p.
    1. Canvas embroidery—Patterns. 2. Design,
Decorative—Plant forms. I. Merrill, Meg, joint
author. II. di Montezemolo, Catherine, joint
author. III. Title. IV. Title: Book of needlepoint.
TT778.C3B6   746.4'4   78-13116
ISBN 0-671-23015-8

To Joe —J.B.
    Si—M.M.
    A. di M.—C. di M.

Acknowledgments

Many people helped in the preparation of this book. Of these, there were four special people whose contribution of time, patience and encouragement went so far above the call of either friendship or obligation that we must mention them individually. These are Kaye Gordon, Joe Leombruno, Barbara Rubinstein and Bob Taylor, all of whom worked countless hours stitching parts of some of the canvases. In addition to stitching, Barbara helped with endless technical problems during the writing and Joe devoted hundreds of hours of his valuable time photographing the finished work. If the book is a success, it will be due in no small part to the assistance we received from these four. To all of them we owe our thanks and give our love.

We also thank Nan Talese and Harriet Ripinsky at Simon and Schuster, Gypsy da Silva, and Jill Weber who graphed the designs.

Contents

Foreword

I saw a delicate flower had grown up two feet high between the horses' feet and the wheel track. An inch more to the right or left had sealed its fate, or an inch higher. Yet it lived to flourish, and never knew the danger it incurred. It did not borrow trouble, nor invite an evil fate by apprehending it.

These few lines by Ralph Waldo Emerson capture a beautifully brave and optimistic outlook on life. It is interesting to realize how often through history many great philosophers and writers have used flowers to express their feelings about life. We can all learn to appreciate the beauty of life more by appreciating the beauty of flowers and plants.

I am an avid gardener and get no greater pleasure than tending my flowers. I feel a part of the earth, a part of all living things. Working outdoors with my hands to care for each flower is very soothing; it makes me feel a part of the earth, in harmony with all living things. In addition, growing different types of flowers, deciding which colors are favorites, and then arranging them throughout the house, can be a wonderful outlet for creativity. An endless number of arrangements can be made by using flowers of various sizes, colors, and shapes.

Which brings me to this charming book. As I think of all the good things flowers can do for people, I realize the amazing similarities between gardening and needlepoint. Needlepoint, too, is a toil of love which uses one's hands in a very delicate way; it is also calming and soothing to the nerves. Needlepoint is a way to bring the garden into your house without being limited by seasons and soil conditions. A garden can be transformed not only into pillows and pictures, but also into vests, bookcovers, slippers, furniture, rugs, pin cushions, eyeglass cases, handbags—an endless variety of objects. Unlike gardening, your needlepoint can go with you everywhere, to pass away your spare time—especially while traveling. It is easily carried in a small bag. I know many famous people, both men and women, doctors, lawyers, and even football players who do needlepoint for pleasure as well as relaxation. I think that people who needlepoint are indeed artists, involving themselves in their intricate creations, just as gardeners dedicate themselves to their flowers. Through needlepoint your whole world can be a garden. Use *A Gardener's Book of Needlepoint* for inspiration and guidance, and let your imagination run wild in deciding what colors, patterns, sizes, shapes, and designs you want to use. In one form or another, gardening has become a lifestyle for many people, and needlepoint is quickly becoming one too. The thought of combining the beauty of flowers with the artistry of needlepoint is one of the best ideas I've ever heard and one that will bring joy and happiness to everyone who does it.

C. Z. GUEST

Introduction

To "all the world loves a lover" might be added "and all lovers love flowers." Children delight in them, they bring cheer to the old and infirm, and brighten the homes of both the rich and the poor. Flowers are nature's jewels in emerald settings.

Anyone who has ever been a gardener—professional or amateur—has experienced the satisfaction of cultivating something that lives and blooms. We hope that this book of "needle gardening" will give you some of the same pleasure. It was conceived to inspire as well as instruct, and to bring out a gardener's creativity. No one person creates the same arrangement of flowers in a vase as the next, neither does she fill a vase one day exactly as she did the day before.

The patterns in these pages give you as much a variety of choice as any vase to be filled. What we earnestly hope is that they will spur you on to create dozens more ideas we haven't even thought of, that it will excite your imagination to take our ideas and create further. Most important, this is a book for those who, whether they garden or not, could not live without the breath of nature the fruits of a garden provide.

1
Materials and Supplies

There is a great variety of materials that can be used in needlepoint and following is a partial list and description of some of them. We have given only a few as it would be impossible to list them all. Throughout the book, we will give the names of books, materials and supplies we have found helpful. A list of them with suppliers' addresses appears in the back.

There is always some confusion as to what is petit point, needlepoint or gros point. All these are needlepoint; the names are simply a clarification of stitch sizes. *Petit* means *small* in French, so petit point is small stitches; *gros* means *large* in French so gros point—or quick point, as it is sometimes called—indicates large stitches. The in-between sizes, worked on 10- through 16-mesh canvases, are simply called needlepoint. Some petit point is done on the finest gauze and, believe it or not, a few people have worked with mercerized cotton, regular sewing thread. We believe it because we have seen it—there are Chinese who work 2,500 stitches per square inch!

You can use textured wools to create dimension and silk, pearl cotton, gold or silver to create highlights. The most important thing to consider when choosing your material is the use of the finished project. Obviously, it is not practical to use a delicate wool or cotton for a rug nor to use rug wool for a pin cushion. Other than that, just about anything goes, although you must be sure the yarn you are using will completely cover the canvas and is not so thick it pushes the canvas threads out of shape or bunches in the holes. You can use yarn made for knitting if you need a color you can't get any other way, but use it only for small areas and never, never for backgrounds. It is too fragile. Experiment on a small piece of canvas if you are not sure how any fiber will work.

We have not listed frames or hoops because to us they are unnecessary, but we know that other, very creative workers do use them.

One of the most essential implements of needlepoint is a pair of small, sharp-pointed and very sharp-bladed scissors. To keep them sharp, use them only to cut your yarn, never paper or canvas.

Some people use thimbles, some don't—even among the three of us. If you are used to sewing with a thimble, you will probably feel naked without one, and you will certainly need one if you find you are constantly poking a hole in your finger. It is important that your thimble fit. Try on different ones until you find one snug enough so you won't be constantly retrieving it from where it has rolled across the floor, yet loose enough so it doesn't stop your blood circulation. Get one with indentations so the needle will not slip against it. For those who have mandarin nails, there is a thimble available that is both practical and beautiful. It fits over the pad and tip of the finger, but is open over the nail.

If you have trouble seeing your work, there are magnifying glasses to hang around your neck, but we think they are awkward. You can also, with the assistance of your optometrist, increase the magnification of your own glasses. Have your doctor give you a prescription for your regular glasses with a bifocal area ground to the magnification that would make the stitches more visible. It works like magic, but use them only when you are stitching.

CANVAS (SCRIM)

MONO.   Mono is single-mesh canvas. Each hole represents one stitch and is called a mesh. In mono canvas, there is only one horizontal and one vertical thread between meshes. If there are 10 meshes to the inch, it is number 10, if there are 12 meshes to the inch, it is number 12; the larger the number the smaller the canvas mesh. Mono canvas is generally woven in widths from 36" to 54" and in white, ecru or beige. All canvas is sold by the yard.

PENELOPE.   Penelope is double-mesh canvas, meaning the vertical threads are paired close together and the horizontal threads have a small space between them. These can be separated to allow for two different stitch sizes on the same piece of work. For example, on 10/20 Penelope, you could have 10 stitches to the inch if you don't separate the threads and 20 stitches to the inch if you do. Most Penelope comes in widths from 36 inches to 40 inches. It is usually in shades of tan, but some places do have it in white.

INTERLOCK.   Interlock is a recent addition to the canvas field; instead of the horizontal and vertical threads crossing each other in a loose, woven pattern as in the other two, interlock has threads that are held tightly in place, with each pair of vertical threads making a half twist around each horizontal. There are several advantages to using this kind of canvas. First, it doesn't ravel so you do not have to bind the edges with masking tape, although it is a good practice to do so because the little points tend to snag wool. Second, it has a more even stitch count than mono and is apt to hold its shape better. Best of all, because it doesn't ravel, if you do the unthinkable and snip a canvas thread while ripping (and who among us hasn't or won't), it is much easier to repair. The disadvantage is that it feels stiffer and has little give, which makes it somewhat more tiring to hold. If you are used to working on mono, you might buy a small piece of interlock to experiment with before making a sizeable investment. Interlock canvas usually comes in widths from 36 inches to 40 inches.

As with any other material, canvas comes in good, less good and absolutely inferior grades. Get the best. Considering the amount of time you will spend on a project, it makes little sense to use a poor quality. One way to tell if the canvas is good is to check the smoothness of the threads. If you see little fuzzy hairs, pass it by. If you see bumps or ties here and there, it is far from the best. Examine the whole piece carefully before it is cut and don't let a smiling persuasive salesperson tell you the bumps don't matter. They do. A tie that seems exceptionally strong when the canvas is new could very easily snap when pressure is put on it during blocking.

MONO

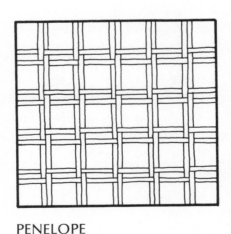

PENELOPE

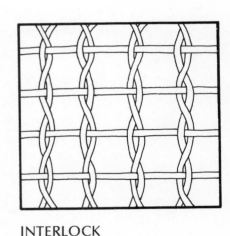

INTERLOCK

WOOL

PERSIAN.   Persian is a three-ply yarn which can be separated very easily into one or two strands for working on meshes above #10 or added to for working on gros point. It is made especially for needlepoint and is a tough, durable wool. Three of our favorite manufacturers of Persian wool are Paternayan, Columbia-

Minerva and DMC. Paternayan Persian comes in 343 colors, Columbia-Minerva in 210 and DMC in 167. Very few shops, if any, have room to store the entire range of colors so you might have to shop around to find exactly the one you want, but with this wealth to choose from, you should find almost any color or shade. Paternayan is sold by weight and in balls of 40 yards and skeins of 8 yards. There are approximately 760 yards in a pound and approximately 47 yards in an ounce. Columbia-Minerva comes in skeins of 25 yards, with some colors available in skeins of 10 yards, and DMC in skeins of 5.4 yards. The skeins are convenient and economical when you need a small amount of one color.

CREWEL.   Crewel is a 2-ply wool, and as its name suggests, it is made especially for crewel embroidery, but it works equally well for needlepoint if you remember that the individual strands are not as thick as Persian. You may need to add a strand to get full coverage. In Paternayan crewel, there are 252 colors. It is sold by weight and in 16 yard skeins. When you need a slightly lighter or darker color and can't find it in Persian, you might be able to get it in crewel.

TAPESTRY.   Tapestry is a 4-ply wool worked as a single ply. It can be separated but only with enormous difficulty plus a good friend to help. Unless there is a color you honestly cannot live without and cannot get any other way, it is best to use it as it comes from the skein. Paternayan tapestry comes in 252 colors, in 8 and 30 yard skeins, all of which match their Persian colors; Columbia-Minerva is available in 54 colors, 40-yard skeins; and DMC is in 430 colors, 8.8 yard skeins. Tapestry covers 12-mesh canvas perfectly, and, if you loosen the stitches slightly, it will cover 10-mesh.

RUG.   Rug wool is a 16-ply yarn worked as a single ply and, as with tapestry, should not be separated. It is used on canvas having a mesh of from 3 to 8, the lowest gauges needing more than one strand. It is extremely durable and the colors are bright and clean. Paternayan rug wool comes in 216 colors. Craft Yarns come in 39 colors. Both are sold by weight only.

Almost all fine wools today are mothproof.

COTTONS AND SILK

All of the cottons listed are made by DMC and are imported from France. If there is a color you want and your shop does not stock it, inquire if it can be specially ordered from France. Some can.

RECTORS À BRODER #4.   This yarn is a single strand, mat finish cotton which is an absolutely perfect medium for working on 14-mesh canvas. The strand fits easily into the hole, lies flat and even and comes in 213 beautiful colors. Threading the needle can be tricky, but pulling an inch or so of the end of the strand between your thumb and the sharp edge of your scissors to fray it slightly takes care of that. Then thread as you do with wool, but put the strand through the eye of the needle carefully or the whole length might fray. It comes in 11-yard skeins.

SIX STRAND FLOSS.   This cotton comes in 320 bright, shiny colors in skeins of 8.7 yards. The strands are easily divided for addition or subtraction. It is an excellent thread to use for highlights; it is easier to use than silk and is much less expensive.

PEARL COTTON.   This is a single strand cotton that comes in bright, clear colors and different thicknesses for stitching on different mesh canvases. As with floss, it can be used to spark highlights. Size 5 comes in 79 colors, in balls of 53 yards and skeins of 27.3 yards. Size 3 comes in 150 colors and skeins of 16.4 yards. Size 8 comes in 138 colors and in balls of 95 yards.

SILK.   Silk is not as easy to work with as wool or cotton, but it is a beautiful fiber and the colors are brilliant and glossy. For the purists who want to use silk for petit point or highlights, there is a Japanese spun silk which comes in 194 breathtaking colors including black and white. It is imported exclusively by Yarn Loft Imports.

QUANTITIES OF YARN

Because the shade of any color may vary slightly from dye lot to dye lot, it is best to buy the right amount of each color at one time. It is better to be on the generous side, although certainly more costly. The following chart will help you accurately determine how many yards or fractions of a yard are needed to cover a square inch with the basketweave stitch on various gauge canvases. If you can estimate how many square inches you need in any one color, simply multiply that by the amount shown on the chart. If you are a novice and unsure of your own calculations, bring the canvas and pattern with you when buying the yarn. Of course, the tension you use as well as the number of times you need to rip must be taken into consideration. You might want to practice doing an inch or so to see if you are getting complete coverage. If you find little flecks of canvas showing through, perhaps you are pulling the thread too tight. You must keep the tension relaxed but even. The strand should lie firm but neither too tight nor too loose on the canvas. If this is not the problem, and the white of the canvas still shows through, perhaps you need to add an extra strand.

CANVAS GAUGE	MATERIAL	LENGTH FOR ONE SQUARE INCH
5	Rug yarn	1 strand, 21"
10	Persian DMC #3 Pearl cotton Tapestry	3 strands, 36" each 2 strands, 40" each 1 strand, 36"
12	Persian DMC #5 Pearl cotton Tapestry Silk	2 strands, 48" each 2 strands, 54" each 1 strand, 50" 4 strands, 50" each
14	DMC mat cotton DMC #3 Pearl cotton Crewel DMC floss	1 strand, 59" 1 strand, 63" 2 strands, 72" each 6 strands, 65" each
16	Persian DMC #5 Pearl cotton DMC floss	1 strand, 78" 1 strand, 73" 4 strands, 72" each
18	Persian DMC #5 Pearl cotton DMC #8 Pearl cotton DMC floss Silk	1 strand, 80" 1 strand, 90" 2 strands, 87" each 4 strands, 84" each 2 strands, 74" each

As you see, the strand lengths will differ with each type of yarn used so check your measurements as you choose materials.

An even easier way to calculate yardage is to get a Tapestry Calculator. With it, you can estimate amounts with amazing accuracy. Its use may seem complicated and time consuming at first, but after using it on several canvases, you will be pleasantly surprised at its speed and simplicity of operation.

OTHER SUPPLIES

NEEDLES. The points of needles used for needlepoint vary in degrees of bluntness. None are as sharp as regular sewing needles; if they were, you would have the devil's own time trying not to split either your canvas, thread or finger. Higher numbered needles have the sharpest points. The size of the needle is determined by the wool used. You don't use a soup ladle to stir your coffee, and you should not use a rug needle to stitch petit point. The proper size needle is important because too large an eye can distort the canvas badly, and the stitches will be uneven. The threaded needle should slip smoothly between the meshes. If you must tug at it to get the thread through, try the next smaller size. If, on the other hand, you simply can't thread a needle, try the next largest. Since there is a certain amount of flexibility in needle size, use the following chart only as a guide for choosing your needles.

CANVAS	NEEDLE
#3 through #5	#13
#7 through #8	#15
#10 through #14	#17 or #18
#16 through #18	#19 or #20
#20 through #32	#21 through #24

To thread the needle, double the strand over the needle and pinch it firmly between the thumb and index finger. Slide the needle out, and the folded end of the yarn will slip easily into the eye.

TWEEZERS. After ripping, you will often have bits of fuzz sticking to the canvas. Unless your nails are very long and pointy, tweezers will come in handy to pick the fuzz off. They will also remove the tiny single "hairs" that will make your work look dirty when you rework the canvas, especially if you are changing colors.

WOOL ORGANIZER. If your wool basket seems to have the same fascinating disarray as that produced by a wind tunnel, there is an inexpensive organizer that will hold small amounts of yarn and keep them separate and untangled. It is called a Yarn Color Organizer. It will hold up to twenty different colors.

2
Beginning a Canvas: Some Rules and Techniques

If you have never worked from a graph, don't be uneasy. Plain canvas takes more attention at first but not the second mortgage or bank loan that is almost required to pay for prepainted canvas.

The difference between working from a graph and following a painted outline is only a matter of counting stitches. Once you get the hang of it, it is not perplexing, and you get a terrific feeling of accomplishment when you have finished.

Before starting to work, draw the heavy grid lines on your canvas as they appear in the graph. These appear every tenth line both vertically and horizontally, and they give a frame of reference as you are stitching. Use a pale gray or tan indelible marker as black could show through your wool—particularly if you are using a white or pastel thread. If you use too pale a color, you will have trouble seeing it. Draw the first vertical line *between* the canvas threads, that is *over the holes*, not on the thread. Count 10 threads and draw another line. Continue until all the vertical lines are drawn. Do the horizontal lines the same way. When you have finished, you will see that each block contains 100 holes. These correspond to the small squares within each larger square on the graph. Mark the top of your canvas. This is to prevent you from angling stitches in the wrong direction when you have to turn your canvas around and work from the bottom as you sometimes will. Count the number of stitches needed for the design you have chosen and draw an outline around the edge.

If you think it would help to color in the graph lightly over the symbols, do it. If you want a colored graph and don't want to deface your book, have a photocopy or a Photostat made and use colored pencils to fill in the copy. This has an added advantage of being easier to tote around than the book.

If you prefer to draw the designs on canvas rather than work them directly from the graphs, have the design photocopied to the size you want. Companies that make Photostats are listed in the Yellow Pages of any telephone directory under Photocopying.

Go over the heavy outlines as we have shown them to make them easier to see through the canvas. Place your canvas over the Photostat, making sure the squared outlines on both are even, and tape them together. Trace the design with a gray or tan marker. You can then color in the Photostat and work from that or paint directly on your canvas. If a shop tells you it is illegal to Photostat the design because of copyright laws, you can explain that it is for your personal use, not for resale, and it is, in fact, legal.

Most important of all is to be sure any medium used to draw or paint on canvas is absolutely, definitely and unconditionally waterproof. Don't take the slightest chance. Be sure. To test any marker, color a small scrap of canvas, let it dry completely, then wash it thoroughly in hot soapy water. If it bleeds the tiniest bit, don't use it as the color will stain your wool during blocking. Jack's designs were drawn and painted with Eberhard Faber's indelible pencils that are specifically designed for needlepoint. They are called Needlepoint Markers. There are only twelve colors, but unless you are doing a lot of complicated and delicate shading, these should be sufficient, particularly since you can use color over color.

In any case, the colors you put on canvas do not have to match the wool exactly. You can approximate the color you are using from these twelve markers, and it will show where your color goes. That is, after all, what you really want to know.

You can also use acrylics. These are water-base plastic paints that dry indelibly. You can mix the colors to get shades you want. Don't mix too much at any one time because they dry quickly and you can't save what you don't use. Put them on the canvas with a light touch; they might clog the holes if the paint is too heavy on the brush or if you use excessive amounts.

Another method is to use oil paint with added Japan drier and greatly thinned with turpentine. Oil colors will soak through to the back of the canvas, so be careful not to paint the canvas on an unprotected piece of furniture. You must wait sometimes as long as forty-eight hours or even longer before oil paints are dry, and they must be *bone* dry before you begin to work. Those who prefer oil paints usually do so because they can be easily mixed into many gradations of color and can be stored indefinitely in jars with tight fitting lids.

There are also two ways to start your first strand. Use the one easiest for you.

1. Put your threaded needle from back to front through the mesh that will be your first stitch. Leave about an inch of yarn hanging loose on the back. Hold this with

your free hand along the line of your stitching and it will be covered and anchored by the first few stitches.

2. Make a knot in the end of your strand. Put your needle through from the front to the back directly in line to the left of and about an inch away from the mesh that will be your first stitch. Leave the knot on the front. After your stitches have covered the strand on the back, snip the knot off from the wrong side.

To end a thread, weave it over and under every other stitch on the wrong side for about an inch. Then clip it very close so there are no stray fibers to be caught in succeeding stitches. Start your next thread with the same weaving on the back.

Strands of Persian and tapestry yarn should be cut about 36 inches long; rug yarn, which is heavier and sturdier, can be somewhat longer, and delicate strands such as crewel, cotton or silk should be shorter.

There are well over a hundred different needlepoint stitches, but we have given directions for only the two which have been used in our stitched designs. You need not be bound by these as many others could be adapted for the patterns. If you have a favorite stitch or one you think is better, by all means, use it.

When Persian wool is purchased by weight, it will usually come loosely knotted in the center. To remove a strand, don't untie the knot. Gently pull a strand from the knot, and it will slip right out, leaving the rest still in one neat bunch. Skeins can be rolled into balls, but wind the wool loosely so as not to stretch it. Keep the identifying number, if you have it, pinned to the wool.

If you are starting your first piece of needlepoint, unless you have the soul of a computer, don't try to interpret the stitch directions by reading alone. The best way to learn correct placement of stitches as well as maintaining an even tension is by practicing on canvas. Before long you will do them without even thinking.

Both the continental and basketweave stitches can be used interchangeably as they look identical on the right side; only the sequence of putting them on canvas is different. The continental should never be used to cover large areas as it will distort the canvas to such an extent that it often is impossible to block it back into shape. Use it only for outlining and for very small areas or a few individual stitches here and there where basketweave is not practical. Always outline blocks of color whether working from a graph or on a painted canvas and then fill in with the basketweave. Outlining from a graph simplifies stitching because if is not necessary to keep referring back for each row, and if you make a mistake, you need only rip a few stitches. When working on a painted canvas, outlining gives you a clearer picture of the design.

Needlepoint has no absolute curves although it appears to. It is a flat plane; the curves are an optical illusion. In continental and basketweave stitches, each individual stitch should sit like a tiny grain of rice tilted upward and to the right, and all should slant in the same direction. The appearance of curves is created by the placement of the stitches. Single lines of stitches slanting from top right to bottom left will have a smooth, joined-together line while those slanting from bottom right to upper left will have a saw-toothed look. The latter is due to the grid of the canvas, so when you see it happening, don't think you are doing something wrong. You will also note that you cannot outline from lower left to top right without turning your canvas around, which is the reason for marking the top of your canvas as we have already mentioned. It must be turned completely around because if you absent-mindedly half turn it, your stitches will slant in the wrong direction.

Next to moth-proofed wool, just about the best thing that has happened to needle-point in the past decade is needlepoint expert Maggie Lane's observation that canvas has a weave. She discovered this quite by accident. If you stitch following her directions, it will result in the wool covering the canvas far more completely and it will help the canvas retain its shape and need very little blocking.

The directions may seem baffling at first . . . they most certainly did to us, but once you master the principle, you will wonder, as Maggie does, why no one ever thought of it before.

When you look closely at mono canvas, you will see that the threads interweave. This means that no two vertical threads, side by side, look exactly alike. One vertical thread goes over the horizontal thread while the vertical thread right next to it goes under the same horizontal thread. When doing the basketweave stitch, anytime the vertical thread is on *top* of the horizontal, you should be stitching the downward angle, that is, your needle comes from under the canvas with its point tilting left. When the vertical thread is *underneath* the horizontal, you should be stitching the upward angle, that is, your needle follows the line of the horizontal thread.

You can start anywhere. The canvas threads will determine whether your second stitch is to the left of the first or below the first. If the directions befuddle you, take a threaded needle and a piece of canvas and follow them step-by-step. It should then be perfectly clear.

To do both the basketweave and continental stitches, follow the charts we have drawn. Stitching in numerical order, use the odd numbers to bring the needle from the back to the front and the even numbers to insert the needle from the front to the back. We have given two drawings showing the placement of stitches depending on the canvas weave for basketweave and one showing how to outline with continental.

While it is certainly true that you can save a considerable amount of money doing your own finishing, here is where lots of experience counts. It is also true that you have spent much money and countless hours of your valuable time stabbing at canvas with your needle, and it would be a shame to ruin it now. Don't do your own finishing if you don't know how to sew. On the other hand, if you think you can do it and want to, a book that will tell you everything you need to know is *Finishing and Mounting Your Needlepoint Pieces,* by Katharine Ireys. You can also buy already made-up pillows which have blank canvas inserted ready to be stitched. One, in particular, that is excellent is called Stitch & Zip. The pillow is completely finished except for the canvas, which zips out. When it has been stitched and inserted, it looks exactly like any professionally completed pillow. It comes in round, square and rectangular sizes and in various colors. There are also trays, boxes, footstools, coasters, etc., using the same technique, and they are quite beautiful and functional. Whoever dreamed those ideas up deserves the thanks of all of us who love needlepointing but who come all over thumbs when it is time to do the finishing.

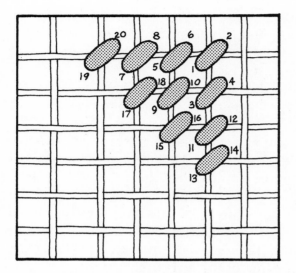

VERTICAL STITCHING BASKETWEAVE   HORIZONTAL STITCHING BASKETWEAVE

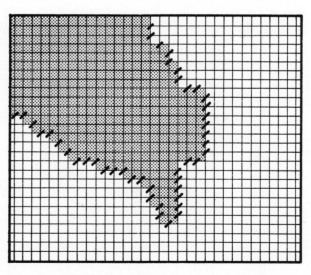

OUTLINING WITH CONTINENTAL

TIPS

If you are a beginning needlepointer, we urge you to practice your stitches before starting to work from a graph. You can make a pillow of different color stripes or squares using the basketweave, and you will acquire an automatic feel for the placement of stitches. You will learn that there is a rhythm in stitching that gives the proper tension for even stitches.

Always leave at least a 2-inch margin of blank canvas around the area to be worked. For large projects, 4 inches is not too much. This allows for the pulling and tugging that takes place during blocking and also gives enough for hemming.

Before starting to work, bind all cut edges with masking or other flexible, sticky tape. An inch-wide tape folded half on the front and half on the back works fine. Some people turn the edges under and stitch them, but we have found tape works best. if your canvas has a selvage edge, keep it vertical as this helps keep the canvas straight. The selvage edge does not need taping.

With an oversize piece of needlepoint, a rug or wall hanging that will need a lot of handling and blocking, sometimes the tape will work loose. Try painting a thin line of watered-down white glue on the cut edges and let it dry completely before taping. This will help stop the canvas from unraveling if the tape loosens.

Always be sure your hands are squeaky clean before beginning to work. Your needlepoint will get enough grime simply sitting around in normal air pollution. There's no need to give it a bad start in life.

Do not, repeat *do not,* work when you are tired, tense or irritated, or when you do not have good light. This may seem casual advice but it isn't unless you enjoy ripping. When you feel your eyes beginning to stand out on stems, no matter how much you want to see how that next stitch will look, just stop. Good light is important not only for proper stitch placement, but also to keep you from eye strain and premature wrinkles in your forehead.

Do not end row after row at the same place. In addition to the ending, you also have to start the next row, and too much starting and stopping in the same place will cause a ridge on the right side of your work. You can correct this by cutting the next few strands a little shorter.

Always give your needle a little twist between your thumb and forefinger as you stitch to keep your wool from bunching. Like telephone cords, thread has a tendency to wind up and twist, and the stitches then become uneven. In addition to the twist, drop the needle every few rows and let it hang free. It will unwind itself.

As wool is an animal fiber, it must breathe. Therefore do not store it over an extended period of time in air tight containers or plastic bags. It will mat and lose its luster without air. It is, however, alright to carry your current project in plastic to keep it clean. This rule does not apply to cotton or silk or man-made fibers.

Do not use too long a strand of wool or, for that matter, any other fiber. The constant pulling through the canvas thins the strands, and the stitches near the end will be flimsy. If you see stitches beginning to look skimpy, end the row and start a new strand.

Most, but not all, wool is colorfast no matter what the label says. But it should never be washed and professional dry-cleaning is not necessary. There are upholstery cleaners that can be sprayed on, which, when dry, turn to a fine white powder which is brushed or vacuumed off. If you find a gritty or sticky residue is left on the surface, remove it with a sponge dampened in a mild solution of ammonia and water. Just wipe the needlepoint gently and rinse out the sponge until it is all off. You can also use a new product called Stitch Clean which comes with a sprayer attachment and is made specially for needlepoint. It will clean without harming wood, plastic or metal.

Keep all your bits and pieces of leftover wool. After all, you've paid practically a king's ransom for them, and if you are not an avid needlepointer when you start, you will more than likely become one. They will be useful in many later projects. We have found it helps to keep the different families of color (see chapter on color) looped together so when you are looking for a particular color, you will have some idea where to find it.

Never try to take a stitch out by pushing your threaded needle back through the hole. The odds are all against you, and the times it will work will only be the exceptions that prove the rule. Unthread your needle and pick the strand through from the back.

If someday you find all the small hairs at the back of your neck rising, your blood beginning to run cold and your nerves curling like bacon over a hot fire, it means you have snipped a canvas thread while ripping. It is not an occasion for joy, but don't panic. There is a remedy. Pull a thread from your canvas near the edge. Very carefully, so as not to unravel the cut thread, remove the stitches all around it. Lay the new canvas thread over the cut extending a few rows vertical or horizontal depending on which thread is cut. Then restitch. It isn't easy, but it works.

Before sending your work out to be finished, or before finishing it yourself, hold the piece up to a strong light. If you have missed any stitches, and no matter how sure you are that you haven't, sometimes you will be startled to find that you have, the light will show through like a tiny flashlight. Give yourself ten demerits and fill them in.

Never end a dark color, if at all possible, by weaving it into a light color. It could show through as a dark shadow on the front. Always weave your beginnings and endings carefully as neatness on the wrong side contributes to smoothness on the right.

Consider putting your initials and/or the date you finished on your work. It is a simple matter to work out your monogram on graph paper, which is easily obtainable in most art supply stores. We have given the name of a place where it can be ordered if your store does not carry it. *Needlepoint Letters and Numbers,* by Carol Cheney Rome and Donna Reedy Orr, contains designs for monograms.

Do not re-use yarn you have ripped unless it is a matter of one or a very few stitches. Ripping is very hard on the strands. When you stitch, you use a sweeping, flowing action of the yarn going through the canvas. Ripping entails too much tugging and pulling, and the yarn becomes frayed, fuzzy and weak.

If you find you have made a terrible mistake, or even a little mistake, particularly in the geometrics, and have to rip, don't feel foolish. Just join the club. Jack has been needlepointing since he was at his mother's knee, and he still rips constantly when doing the designs. He doesn't like it a lot, but he does it as we all do. Go on and shed bitter tears, if you must, but don't leave mistakes in. You will never be happy with the finished work.

There are any number of ways to rip. You can use your needle to pick out the stitches, which is not difficult if you have stitched carefully and not split your stitches. You can cut the stitches with your scissors, but it must be done with extreme caution so as not to cut the canvas along with the wool. Then there is a marvelous little gadget called a Stitch-Pic that will both pick the stitches out and also cut them. It has a handle much like a pen and is far easier on the fingers than a needle, but you must be careful only to pull at the wool and not the canvas.

Sometimes a finished piece will appear to have a hairy look, which comes from small fibers of the wool sticking out due to constant handling. This can be corrected easily if you have a steady and sure hand and great courage. Just light a match, preferably a wooden one, hold it near but not on the needlepoint and move it rapidly back and forth. All those little hairs will disappear, and in their place will be small, shriveled fibers which can then be brushed off.

3
Adaptation
of Color

Color is very much a matter of personal taste. One person's elegance is another person's migraine. In spite of what you may have been told to the contrary, there are no hard and fast rules that make one combination of colors right and another wrong. There are, indeed, popular or fashionable colors, but they constantly change. Use the colors that please you and those with whom you live, or please the people to whom you will give gifts of your work. Not everyone is excited by the same colors; it would be a tiresome and drab world if they were. Having said all that, however, we must point out that there are some colors that combine better than others. When you choose wool for needlepoint, it is essential to keep in mind that colors of equal tonal value (the degree of lightness or darkness) used in the same amounts, or sometimes not even in the same amounts next to each other will almost always give the effect of one color. Be exceedingly careful about this. It is much better to find it out when the wool is in your hand than it is when the wool is in your canvas. If you are unsure, don't hesitate to ask lots of questions where you buy your wool. Generally, the owner and personnel in needlepoint shops are stitchers themselves and will be happy to advise you. After all, they want you as a steady customer.

Some brilliant colors of the same intensity will "move" when they are side by side; for example, kelly green and geranium red. Artists have used this to great effect in optical illusions, and there is no reason not to get this result if that is what you are after, but do it deliberately, not by mistake.

Before making your color decision, hold hanks of wool together in your hand in both daylight and artificial light as the colors often appear very different under different lights. You can also hold two or three strands of wool in each color twisted together. If they seem to blend, you need to change the value of one.

All the colors Jack has chosen for our designs have been taken directly from nature even though they are, in some cases, more exotic, whimsical, and vibrant; and there is no better place than nature to go for inspiration. If you look at the produce display in any market, except those dreadful places that package everything tightly in plastic, you will see how natural colors inspire you to create stunning color relationships.

When choosing your background color, remember that light colors advance and dark colors recede. If the design is light, it should sit on a darker background; if it is dark it will pop out of a light background. Unstitched wool is loose and round, but on the canvas it is tight and flat and therefore colors always appear somewhat darker when stitched than they do in the skein. It is important to remember this in case you find, as sometimes happens to the best of us, that you have run out of wool. You must take a strand or two of the wool to the store and not the stitched piece. Some colors are much too close in value to be matched without the actual thread. Most manufacturers give their yarns numbers. Some have added names. When buying your material, if your store is friendly, ask to have the catalog number of the yarn and keep a record of it.

The most important area to consider when buying wool is the background. It is better to get too much than too little. If you have some left over, you can always use it in a future project. In small, broken-up areas, a tiny color variation will not show, and dye lots match much closer now than they did in your grandmother's day. Still, even a whisper of a difference will show in a fiendish way in the background, and you will not notice it until you have stitched it, when it is sort of like finding a centipede in your stocking. Even then, if the worst happens, and you find you have run out of wool, there is a remedy. When you realize you need more, save the last few strands. Use two strands from the original batch and one from the new. Stitch a few rows with this, then use one strand from the old and two from the new. Finally use only the new. This blending will usually keep the difference in dye lots from being too apparent, if visible at all. Naturally, this works only with wool that can be easily separated such as Persian, crewel, or 6-strand cotton. It will not work with rug yarn, tapestry wool or single-strand cotton. For these it is imperative to buy enough in the beginning.

When choosing colors, consider the colors in the room where your finished piece will find its home. Don't be afraid to use color. Think of your design as the star and the colors as the supporting cast. You will have worked long and hard on your needlepoint. You want to show it off, but if you use gloomy or dull colors, it will sink like a blob into the background and no one will notice it.

Both wool and cotton colors come in an exciting wealth of marvelous shades and tints. If you have no idea which ones to use, go into any shop that carries a fairly complete selection and look in the bins. Your problem then will likely be which to eliminate. You will probably love them all.

Colors are spoken of as belonging to "families," that is related colors from dark shades to light tints with each having the same color make-up such as purple-red, orange-red, pure red and so on. There are even whites that belong in different families. One will belong with a warm yellow family, for example, another with a cool blue and still another with the grays. Paternayan has nine whites, including a pure white. The same is true with black. Some are green-black, some are blue-black. There is a black-black, but unless there is some intentional reason for using this, the others look much better. The true black has a lifeless quality and even feels harsh to the touch.

Some companies have as many as seven colors in a single family. If you can't find a color that is only a little lighter or darker to fit in with a group you are using, try another brand. You can also change the color slightly by taking one strand from the lighter and one from the darker color or, if you are using three strands, two from one and one from the other. Just be sure when shading that your color families match.

Using these wheels as guides, let your imagination soar.

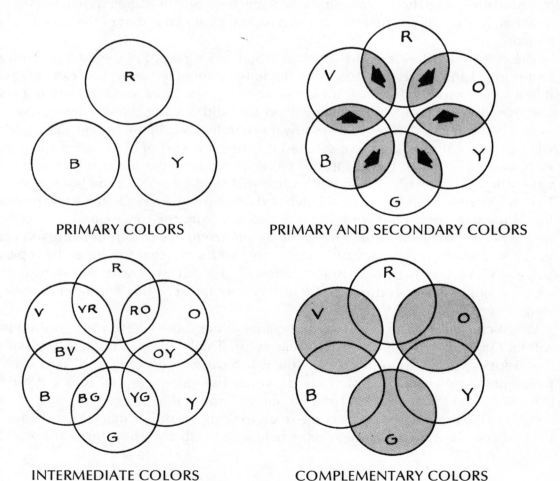

PRIMARY COLORS   PRIMARY AND SECONDARY COLORS

INTERMEDIATE COLORS   COMPLEMENTARY COLORS

4
Filling Containers with Flowers and Vegetables

CHINESE CACHEPOT

The cachepot has been designed to be filled with either of two bouquets, which gives an idea of the variety of effects that can be accomplished with a single vase. If you use your own individual flower arrangement, be sure that the leaves and flowers that spill over are substituted with similar abundance, filling the exact areas, but in your own design.

Using #10 mono canvas, the stitched area will measure 17½ inches square. There are 173 by 173 stitches in the square.

Cut a piece of canvas 21½ inches square. Mark the heavy graph lines on the canvas as shown on the graph, and draw the outline of the square. Mark the top of the canvas.

The letters P and C-M next to the color numbers indicate Paternayan and Columbia-Minerva wools respectively. The colors as they appear in the photographs are:

⊠	CORNFLOWER BLUE	P 731
	CORNFLOWER BLUE	C-M 731
▨	MEDIUM BLUE	P 733
	MEDIUM BLUE	C-M 752
⧄	MISTY BLUE	P 741
	MISTY BLUE	C-M 741
⊡	SUMMER BLUE	P 743
	SUMMER BLUE	C-M 756
☐	WHITE	P 001
	WHITE	C-M 005

CHINESE CACHEPOT WITH BLUE FLOWERS AND LEAVES

FLOWERS AND LEAVES

■	DARK BLUE DARK BLUE	P 721 C-M 740
⊠	CORNFLOWER BLUE CORNFLOWER BLUE	P 731 C-M 731
▨	MEDIUM BLUE MEDIUM BLUE	P 733 C-M 752
◪	MISTY BLUE MISTY BLUE	P 741 C-M 741
J	GYPSY BLUE GYPSY BLUE	P 611 C-M 611
⊡	SUMMER BLUE SUMMER BLUE	P 743 C-M 756
◢	DARK GREEN DARK GREEN	P 524 C-M 524
+	BRILLIANT GREEN BRILLIANT GREEN	P 559 C-M 559
−	APPLE GREEN APPLE GREEN	P 569 C-M 569
S	LIGHT APPLE GREEN LIGHT APPLE GREEN	P G-74 C-M G-74
H	SPRING GREEN SPRING GREEN	P 575 C-M 575
☐	WHITE WHITE	P 001 C-M 005

CHINESE CACHEPOT

⊠	CORNFLOWER BLUE CORNFLOWER BLUE	P 731 C-M 731
▨	MEDIUM BLUE MEDIUM BLUE	P 733 C-M 752
◪	MISTY BLUE MISTY BLUE	P 741 C-M 741
⊡	SUMMER BLUE SUMMER BLUE	P 743 C-M 756
☐	WHITE WHITE	P 001 C-M 005

Geometric Pattern

⊡	SUMMER BLUE SUMMER BLUE	P 743 C-M 756
◪	MISTY BLUE MISTY BLUE	P 741 C-M 741

Overall Background

☐	WHITE WHITE	P 001 C-M 005

THESE 10 SQUARES ARE REPEATED

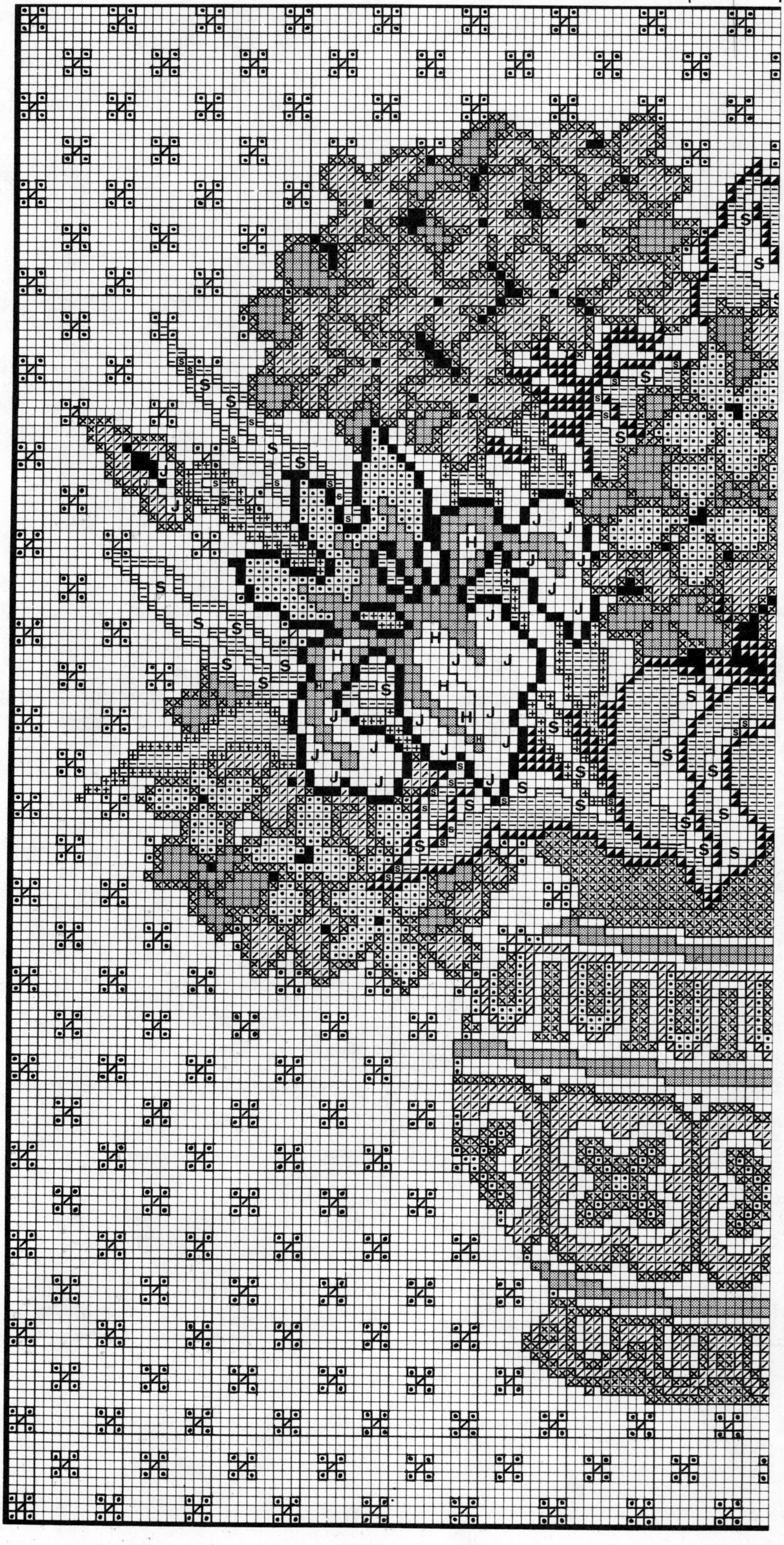

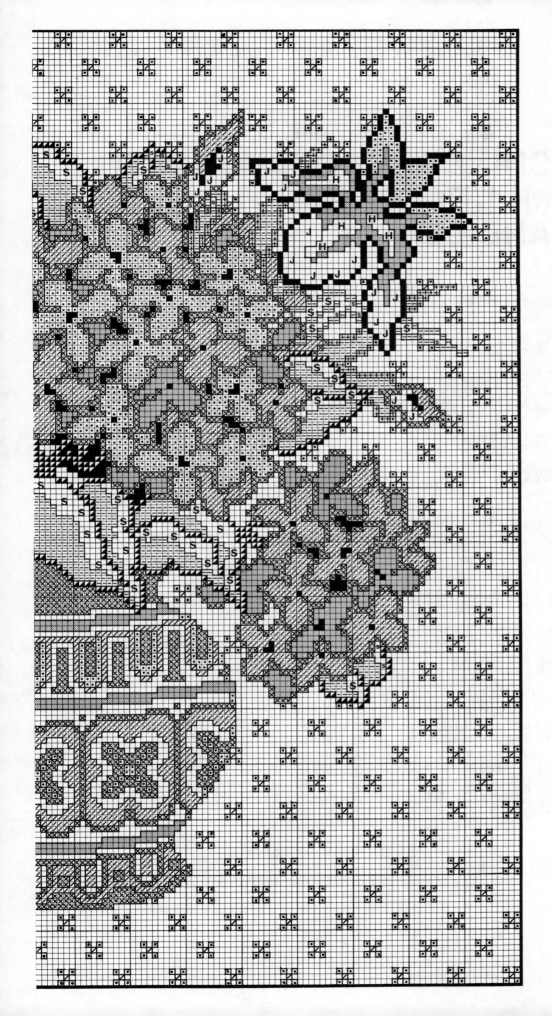

CHINESE CACHEPOT WITH MULTICOLORED FLOWERS AND LEAVES

FLOWERS AND LEAVES

■	BRIGHT PURPLE BRIGHT PURPLE	P 642 C-M 642
J	LIGHT PURPLE LIGHT PURPLE	P 650 C-M 650
◉	MAGENTA MAGENTA	P 623 C-M 639
=	FUCHSIA DAZZLE	P 644 C-M 645
Ⓞ	MEXICAN PINK MEXICAN PINK	P 828 C-M 828
H	FLESH FLESH	P 992 C-M 853
◿	RED RED	P 242 C-M 242
Ⓞ	SUMMER ORANGE SUMMER ORANGE	P 968 C-M 968
I	PUMPKIN SEED PUMPKIN SEED	P Y-40 C-M 975
⊓	CANARY YELLOW CANARY YELLOW	P Y-44 C-M 457
B	LIGHT YELLOW LIGHT YELLOW	P 452 C-M 452
◢	DARK GREEN DARK GREEN	P 524 C-M 524
+	BRILLIANT GREEN BRILLIANT GREEN	P 559 C-M 559
−	APPLE GREEN APPLE GREEN	P 569 C-M 569
S	LIGHT APPLE GREEN LIGHT APPLE GREEN	P G-74 C-M G-74

CHINESE CACHEPOT

⊠	CORNFLOWER BLUE CORNFLOWER BLUE	P 731 C-M 731
▦	MEDIUM BLUE MEDIUM BLUE	P 733 C-M 752
◿	MISTY BLUE MISTY BLUE	P 741 C-M 741
⊡	SUMMER BLUE SUMMER BLUE	P 743 C-M 756
☐	WHITE WHITE	P 001 C-M 005

Geometric Pattern

⊡	SUMMER BLUE SUMMER BLUE	P 743 C-M 756
◿	MISTY BLUE MISTY BLUE	P 741 C-M 741

Overall Background

☐	WHITE WHITE	P 001 C-M 005

46

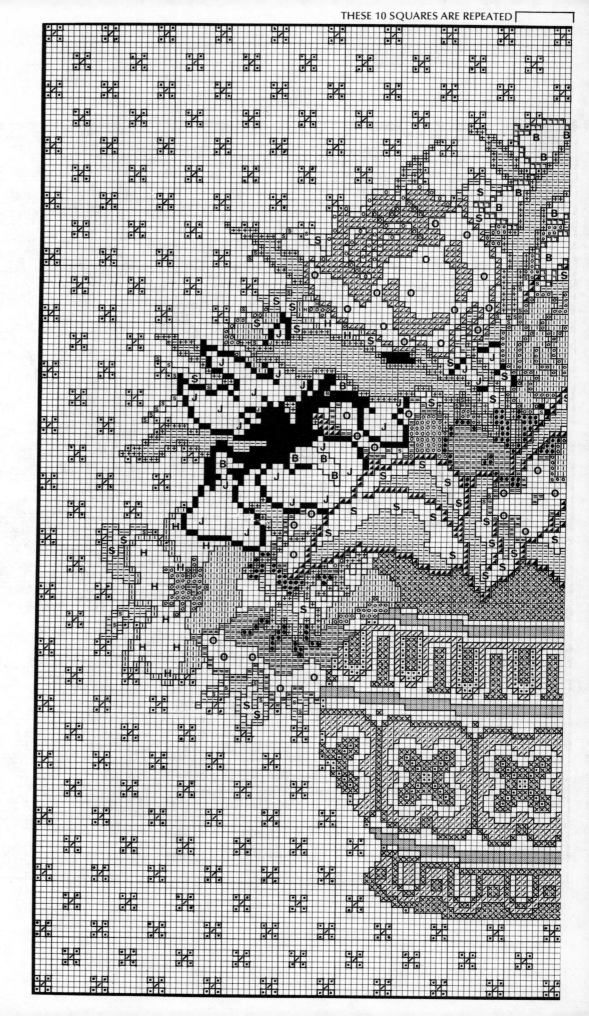

BASKET WITH VEGETABLE OR FLOWER FILLER

Filling a basket with fruits, flowers and vegetables has always seemed the very essence of summer. This basket, filled, would make a handsome banquette pillow or wall hanging, or on a lower gauge canvas, a beautiful rug. You can also substitute your own arrangement.

Using #10 mono canvas, the stitched area will be 22½ by 16 inches. There are 224 by 161 stitches in the rectangle.

Cut a piece of canvas 26½ by 20 inches. Mark the heavy graph lines on the canvas as shown on the graph, and draw the outline of the square edge. Mark the top of the canvas.

The colors of the design as shown in the color photograph are listed below. We have listed only Paternayan wools because there is no exact match in Columbia-Minerva.

The colors as they appear in the photographs are:

BASKET

S	DARK BROWN	P 145
■	MEDIUM BROWN	P 462
▨	LIGHT BROWN	P 492

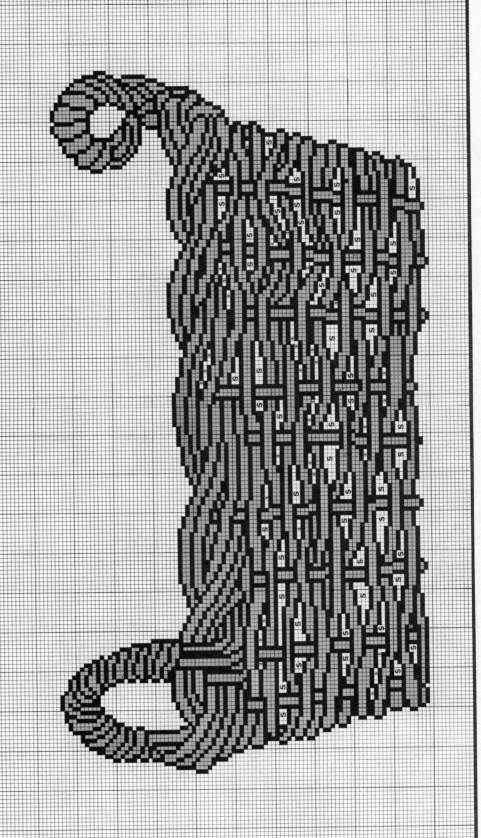

VEGETABLE FILLER

Symbol	Color	Code
◹	BURNT ORANGE	P 960 / C-M 960
T	LIGHT ORANGE	P 970 / C-M 970
⌷	PUMPKIN SEED	P Y-40 / C-M 975
B	YELLOW	P 450 / C-M 450
=	INDIGO	P 640 / C-M 640
G	BRIGHT PURPLE	P 642 / C-M 642
A	LILAC	P 652 / C-M 652
J	PALE MAUVE	P 229 / C-M 229
◿	PURPLE CLARET	P 221 / C-M 221
H	FUCHSIA DAZZLE	P 644 / C-M 645
●	MISTY BLUE	P 741 / C-M 741
E	SUMMER BLUE	P 743 / C-M 756
◣	HUNTER GREEN	P 520 / C-M 520
X	MEDIUM GREEN	P 510 / C-M 510
–	GREEN GIANT	P 555 / C-M 555
+	DARK GREEN	P 524 / C-M 524
/	SPRING APPLE GREEN	P G-64 / C-M G-64
—	SEAWEED	P 574 / C-M 574
·	LIGHT APPLE GREEN	P G-74 / C-M G-74
⊙	CRANBERRY	P 240 / C-M 240
C	TRUE RED	P R-10 / C-M R-10
D	DARK ORANGE	P 958 / C-M 958
☐	WHITE	P 001 / C-M 005

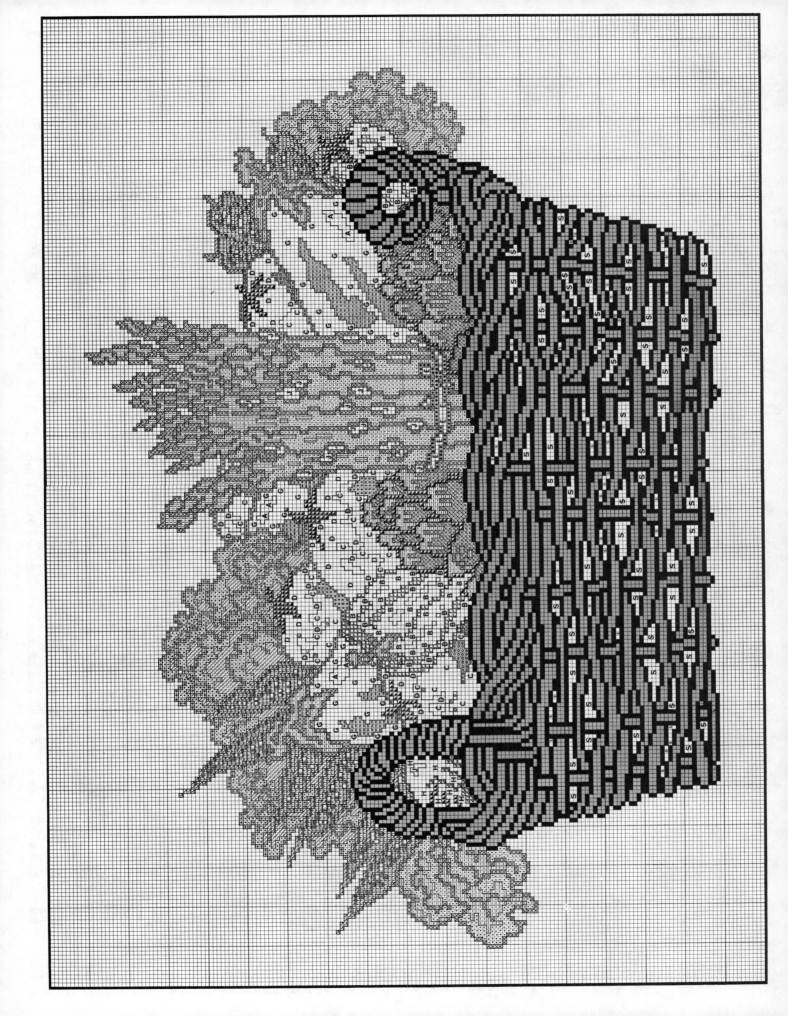

THESE 10 SQUARES ARE REPEATED

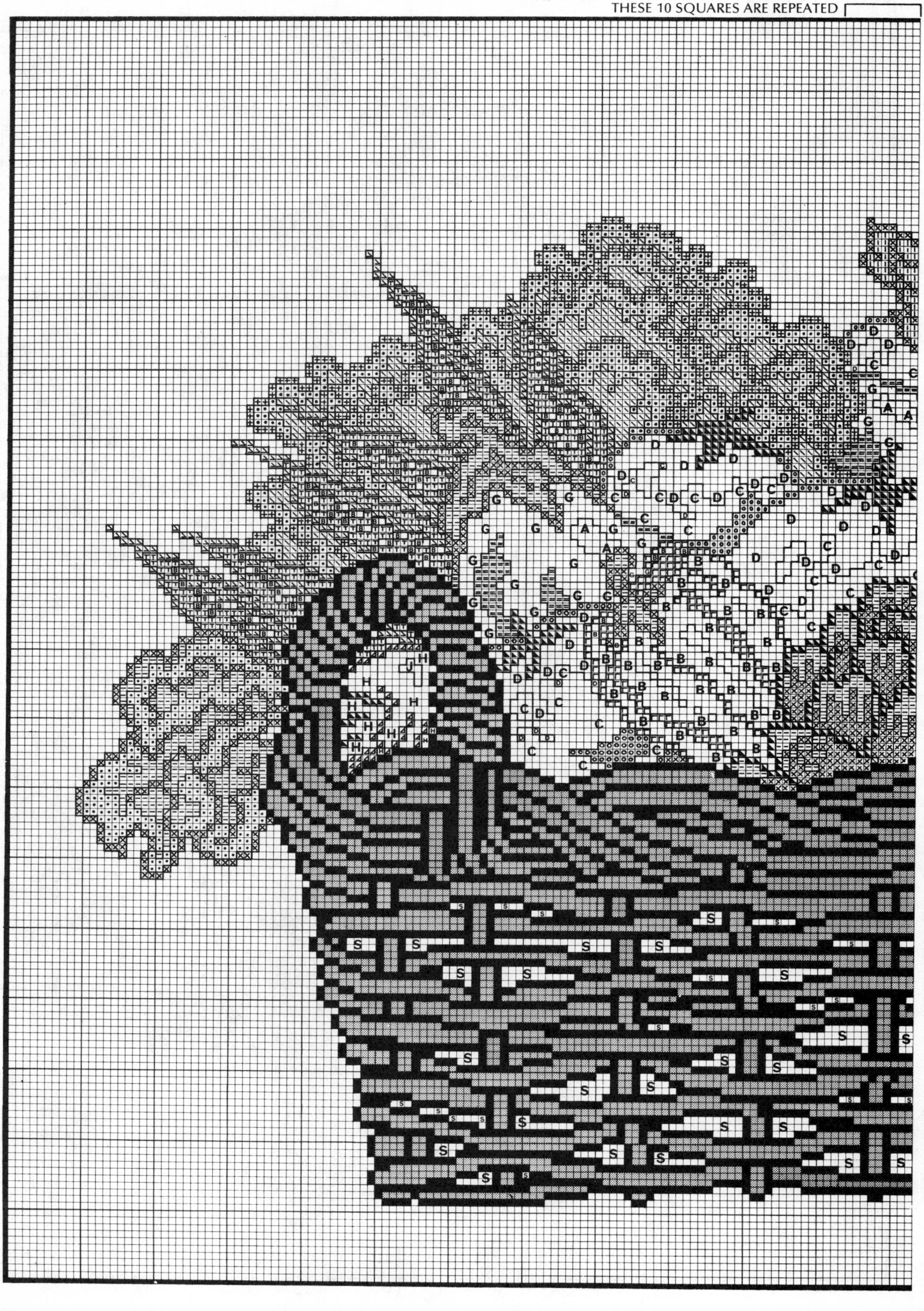

FLOWER FILLER

Symbol	Color	Code
◤	FOREST GREEN / FOREST GREEN	P 528 / C-M 528
⊠	BRILLIANT GREEN / BRILLIANT GREEN	P 559 / C-M 559
◩	APPLE GREEN / APPLE GREEN	P 569 / C-M 569
−	LIGHT APPLE GREEN / LIGHT APPLE GREEN	P G-74 / C-M G-74
+	DARK ORANGE / DARK ORANGE	P 958 / C-M 958
A	CARROT / CARROT	P 965 / C-M 965
·	PUMPKIN SEED / PUMPKIN SEED	P Y-40 / C-M 975
◎	YELLOW / YELLOW	P 450 / C-M 450
⊘	CORNFLOWER BLUE / CORNFLOWER BLUE	P 731 / C-M 731
B	MISTY BLUE / MISTY BLUE	P 741 / C-M 741
L	BRIGHT PURPLE / BRIGHT PURPLE	P 642 / C-M 642
J	LIGHT PURPLE / LIGHT PURPLE	P 650 / C-M 650
●	MAGENTA / MAGENTA	P 623 / C-M 639
−	TRUE RED / TRUE RED	P R-10 / C-M R-10
◎	FUCHSIA / DAZZLE	P 644 / C-M 645
=	CERISE / CERISE	P 649 / C-M 827
D	MEXICAN PINK / MEXICAN PINK	P 828 / C-M 828
G	BLACK / BLACK	P 304 / C-M 050
□	WHITE / WHITE	P 001 / C-M 005

THESE 10 SQUARES ARE REPEATED

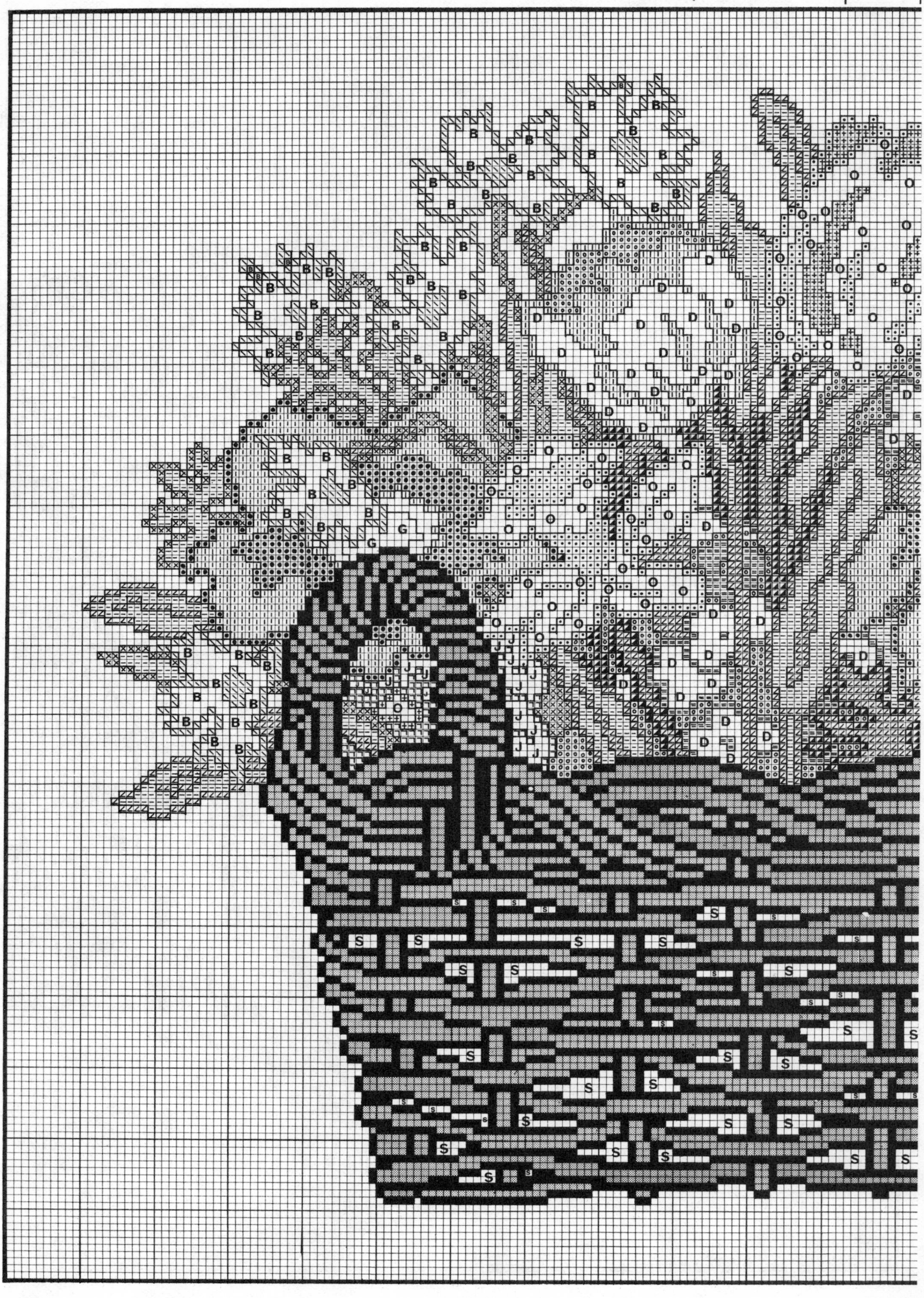

CLAY POT WITH CALADIUM OR GERANIUM

This simple pot may be filled with a variety of ferns and plants, stitched into a single pillow, or made into a series that we show with a caladium and a geranium, and can go on through a succession of blossoming and green plants.

Using #10 mono canvas, the stitched area will be 14 by 14 inches. there are 140 by 140 stitches in the square.

Cut a piece of canvas 18 by 18 inches. Mark the heavy graph lines on the canvas as shown on the graph, and draw the outline of the square edge. Mark the top of the canvas.

The colors of the design as shown in the color photographs are listed below. The letters P and C-M next to the color numbers indicate Paternayan and Columbia-Minerva wools respectively.

Note: Jack has designed the pot so it "sits" on the bottom of the canvas. If you prefer to have background all around, add another 10 stitches to the length.

CLAY POT

☒	WOOD BROWN WOOD BROWN	P 217 C-M 217
☐B	RUST RUST	P 414 C-M 414
☐D	FLESH FLESH	P 992 C-M 853

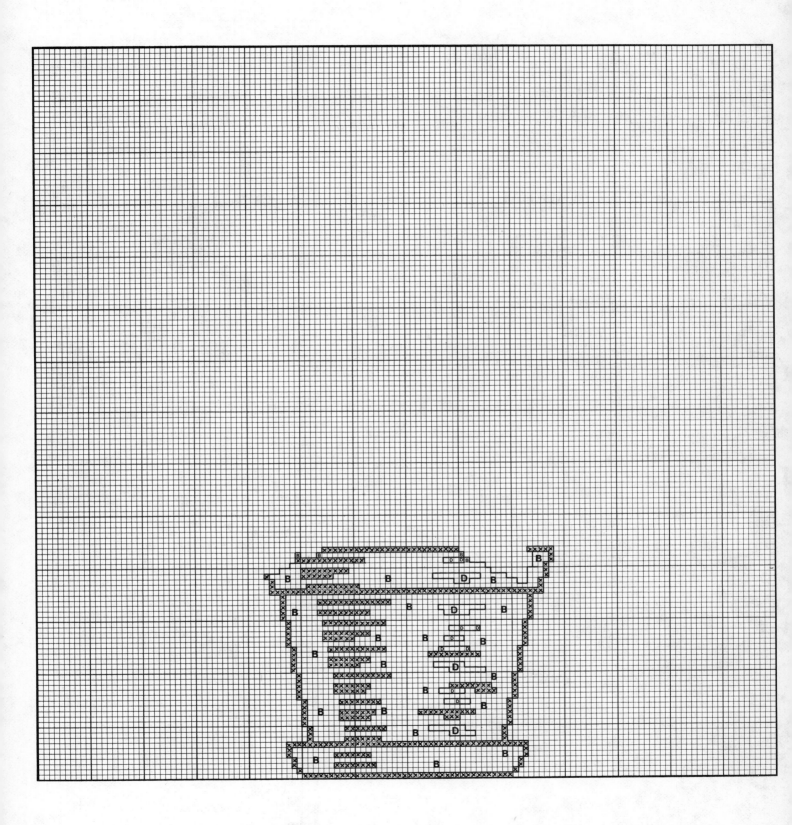

THESE 10 SQUARES ARE REPEATED

CALADIUM

	HUNTER GREEN	P 520
■	HUNTER GREEN	C-M 520
⊡	BRILLIANT GREEN	P 559
	BRILLIANT GREEN	C-M 559
▨	LIGHT APPLE GREEN	P G-74
	LIGHT APPLE GREEN	C-M G-74
□	WHITE	P 001
	WHITE	C-M 005

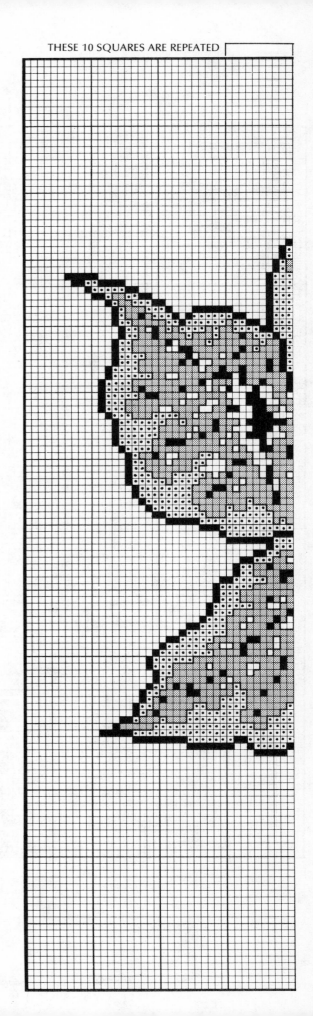

62

GERANIUM

	CRANBERRY	P 240
	CRANBERRY	C-M 240
	TRUE RED	P R-10
	TRUE RED	C-M R-10
C	DARK ORANGE	P 958
	DARK ORANGE	C-M 958
	HUNTER GREEN	P 520
	HUNTER GREEN	C-M 520
+	MEDIUM GREEN	P 510
	MEDIUM GREEN	C-M 510
E	GREEN GIANT	P 555
	GREEN GIANT	C-M 555
	LIGHT APPLE GREEN	P G-74
	LIGHT APPLE GREEN	C-M G-74
	WHITE	P 001
	WHITE	C-M 005

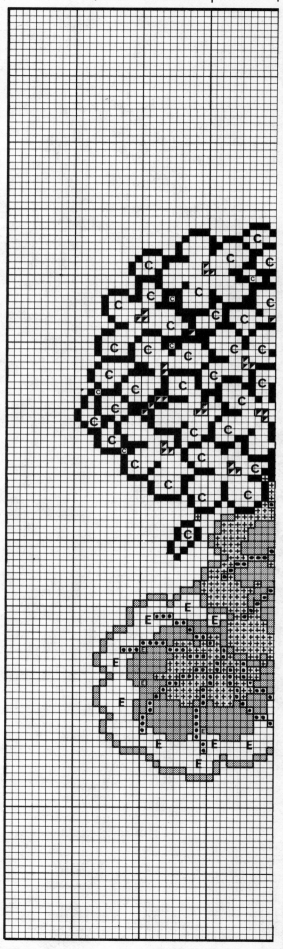

5
Border Planting

Borders around centered pieces of needlework are as elegant as borders planted around a formal garden. In the following canvases nature provides the runners of strawberries, but whimsy encircles a large tulip with gingham. Some patterns from the backgrounds of the alphabet are included to be used with whatever colors are in your canvas.

STRAWBERRIES

Cut the #10 mono canvas 18¾ inches by 18½ inches. The finished canvas will measure 14¾ by 14⅓ and the stitched area will have 148 by 143 stitches. The following colors were used:

⊞	CRANBERRY CRANBERRY	P 240 C-M 240	⊡ SPRING APPLE GREEN SPRING APPLE GREEN	P G-64 C-M G-64
◻	CERISE CERISE	P 649 C-M 827	Ⓐ PUMPKIN SEED PUMPKIN SEED	P Y-40 C-M 975
▦	MEXICAN PINK MEXICAN PINK	P 828 C-M 828	◻ WHITE WHITE	P 001 C-M 005
◼	BRILLIANT GREEN BRILLIANT GREEN	P 559 C-M 559		

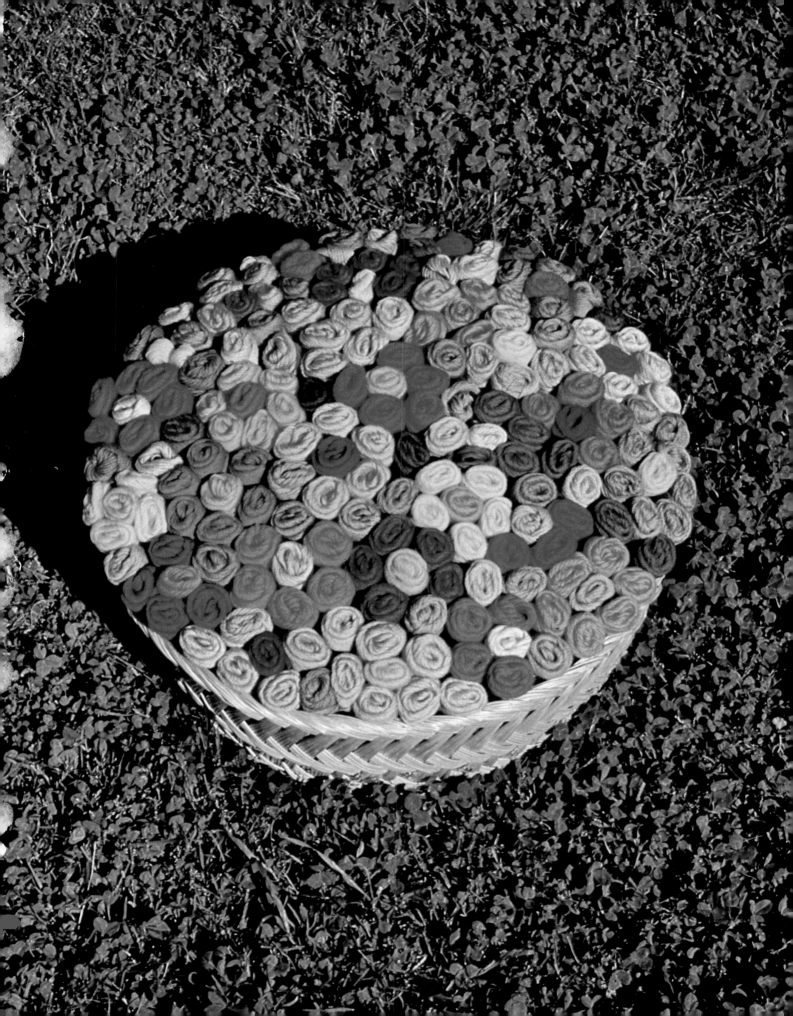

page 38

page 44

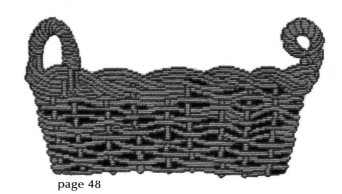

page 48

page 50

page 54

page 58

page 60

page 64

page 68

page 144

page 140

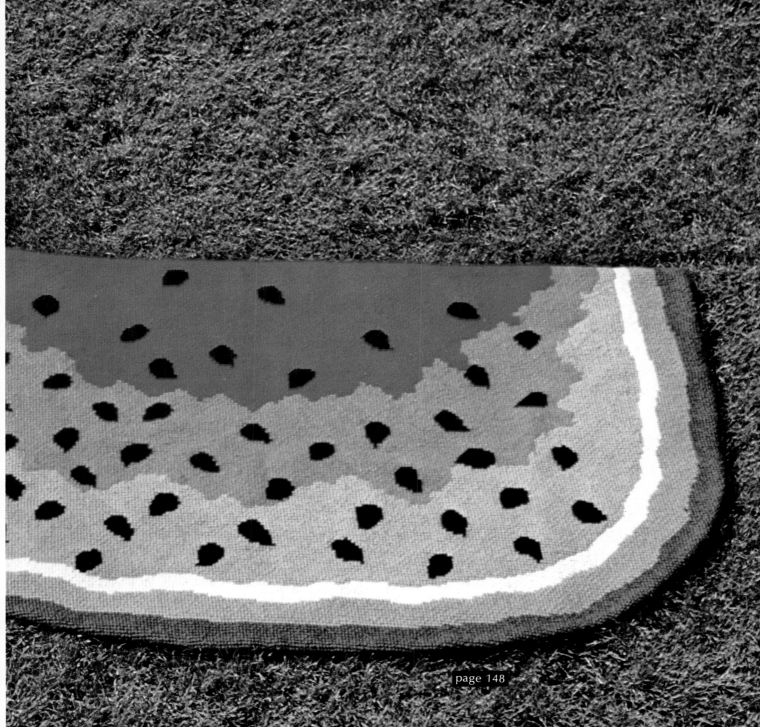

page 148

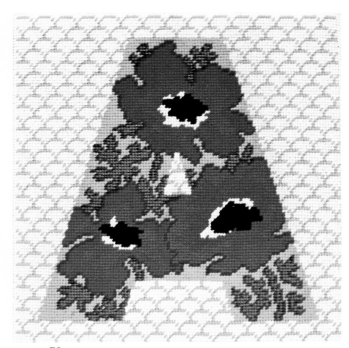

page 78

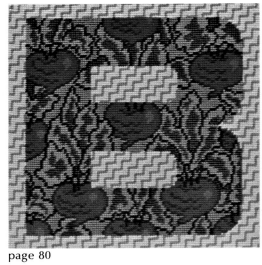

page 80

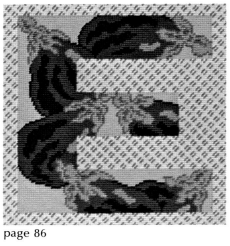

page 86

page 88

page 94

page 82

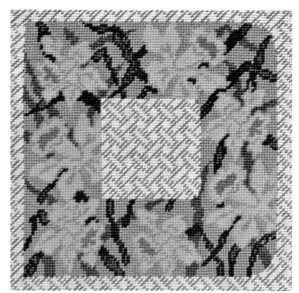
page 84

page 90

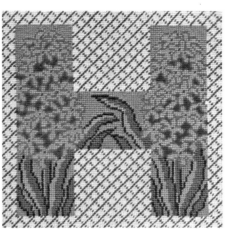
page 92

page 96

page 98

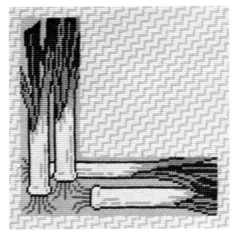

page 100

page 102

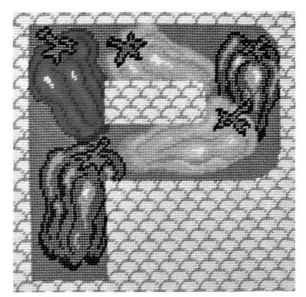

page 108

page 110

page 116

page 104

page 106

page 112

page 114

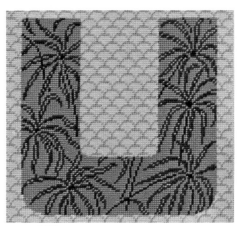

page 118

page 120

page 122

page 124

page 126

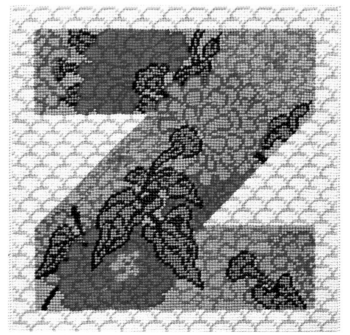

page 128

66

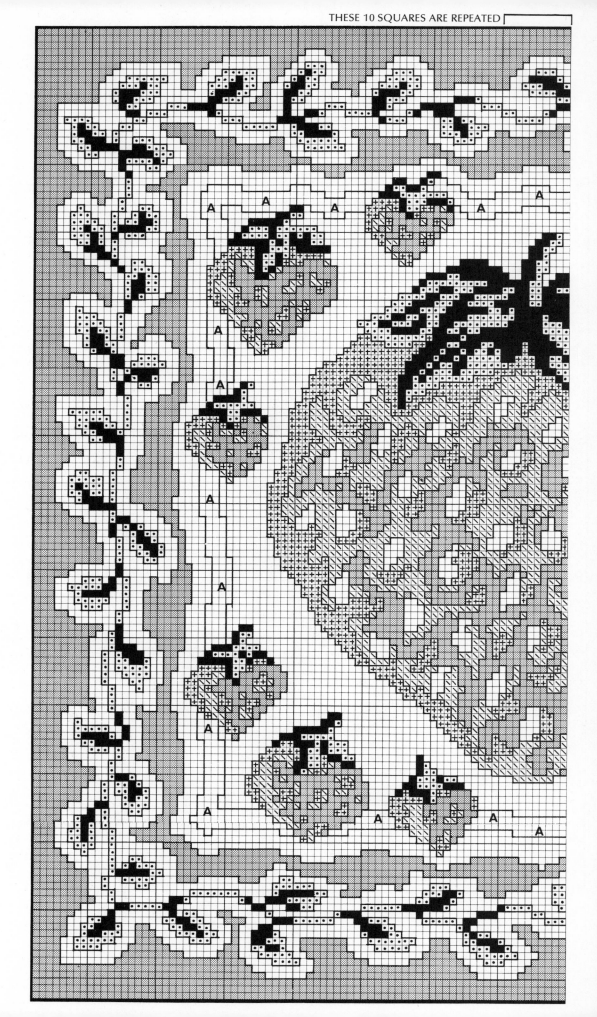

A BUNCH OF CARROTS

On a #10 mono canvas, the stitched area will measure 14¾ by 14½. The stitched area has 148 stitches by 144 stitches. Cut the canvas 18¾ inches by 18½ inches. The following colors were used:

	Color	Code
⊙	YELLOW YELLOW	P 450 C-M 450
D	LIGHT ORANGE LIGHT ORANGE	P 970 C-M 970
■	BURNT ORANGE BURNT ORANGE	P 960 C-M 960
⊞	CRANBERRY CRANBERRY	P 240 C-M 240
E	TRUE RED TRUE RED	P R-10 C-M R-10
◩	PALE MAUVE PALE MAUVE	P 229 C-M 229
⊠	DARK GREEN DARK GREEN	P 524 C-M 524
⊟	SPRING APPLE GREEN SPRING APPLE GREEN	P G-64 C-M G-64
⊡	LIGHT APPLE GREEN LIGHT APPLE GREEN	P G-74 C-M G-74
▦	CORNFLOWER BLUE CORNFLOWER BLUE	P 731 C-M 731
◥	MISTY BLUE MISTY BLUE	P 741 C-M 741
A	PALE RUST PALE RUST	P 423 C-M 423
◤	TOBACCO TOBACCO	P 145 C-M 145
□	WHITE WHITE	P 001 C-M 005

70

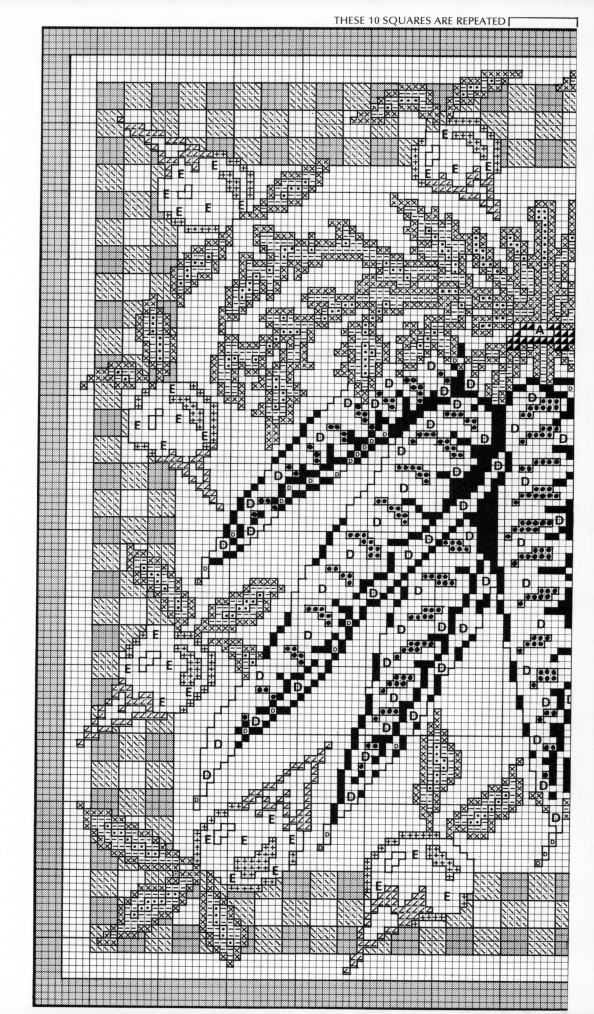

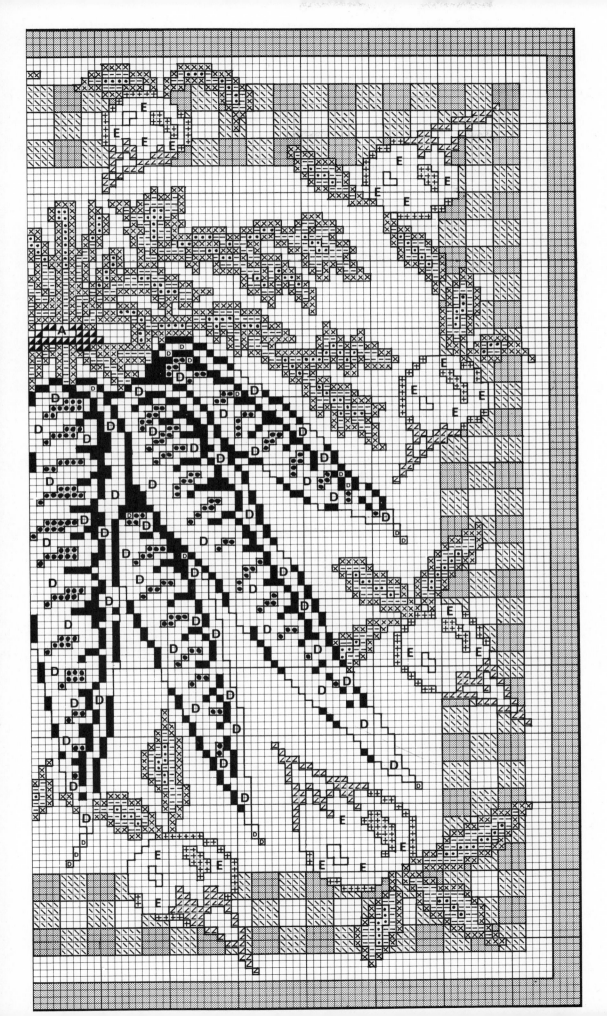

TULIP WITH GINGHAM

Cut the #10 mono canvas 29 inches by 49 inches. The finished canvas will measure 25 inches by 45 inches, and the stitched area will have 251 stitches by 450 stitches. The following colors were used:

⊡	TRUE RED TRUE RED	P R-10 C-M R-10
⊠	BRIGHT PURPLE BRIGHT PURPLE	P 642 C-M 642
▦	PUMPKIN SEED PUMPKIN SEED	P Y-40 C-M 975
◿	YELLOW YELLOW	P 450 C-M 450
■	BRILLIANT GREEN BRILLIANT GREEN	P 559 C-M 559
⊡	SPRING APPLE GREEN SPRING APPLE GREEN	P G-64 C-M G-64
☐	WHITE WHITE	P 001 C-M 005

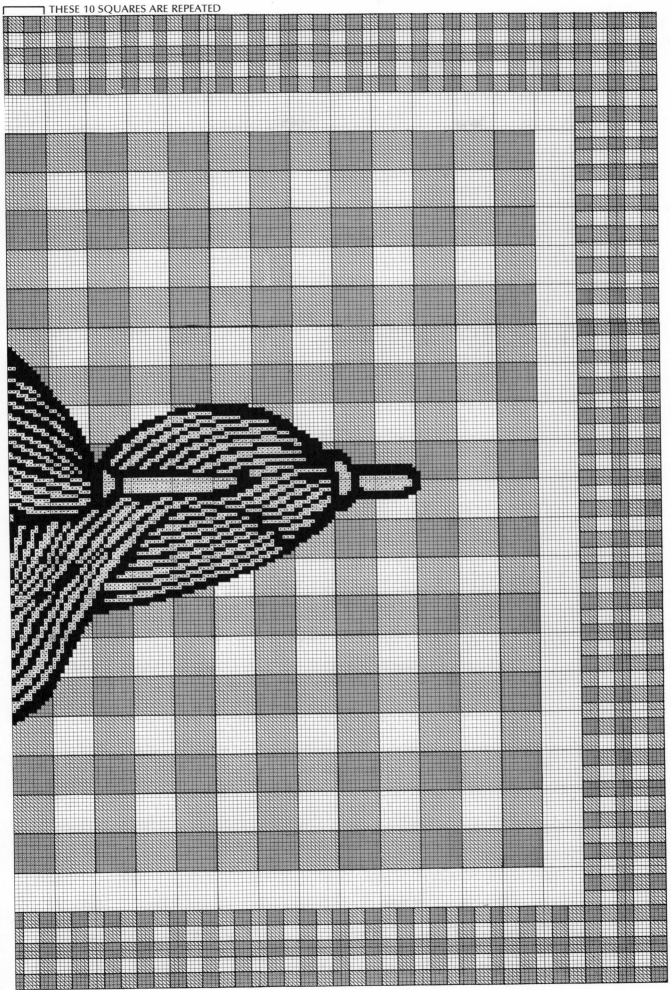

6
The Greening of the Alphabet

We have chosen the flowers, fruits and vegetables that we like to match the alphabet letters, but there are dozens more than can fit equally well. If you prefer a rose rather than a radish for the "R" and want to change it, you can trace a pattern from the flower books we have listed in the Bibliography—or draw your own.

In addition, in order for you to be able to change the colors we have used so you can more nearly match your own color scheme, we have tried to give all the colors and color combinations that are natural to each flower. Most will be familiar, but some may surprise you as they did us when we were doing the research. Although there is no pure black or white in nature (with the exception of true albinos and snow), you will note that we have used some pure white because although the designs are realistic in shape, the shadings and, in many cases, the colors are stylized. Of course, if you want to make a flower in a color that is totally unnatural to it, a fantasy color so to speak, it could be striking, How about a pale blue Queen Anne's lace or most delicate of green mushrooms?

All of the letters have the same stitch count around the square so if you want to use two or more together for a rug or wall hanging, you will not have to revise the sizes. The backgrounds can be extended using either a plain color, the same geometric pattern, or a contrasting border (see page 130). A pillow can be made with a geometric pattern overall to pair with a letter with a matching background in either the same or complementary colors.

Using #10 mono canvas, the stitched area will be 11½ inches by 11½ inches. There are 116 stitches by 116 stitches in the square.

Cut a piece of canvas 15½ inches by 15½ inches. Mark the heavy graph lines on the canvas as shown on the graph and draw the outline of the square. Mark the top of the canvas.

The colors of the design as shown in the color photographs are listed. The letters P and C-M next to the numbers indicate Paternayan and Columbia-Minerva wool respectively.

A rug made from all of the alphabet letters would be stunning. To make one you would need to space four letters as the top (A, B, C and D) and bottom rows (W, X, Y and Z) with six letters on each of the three center rows across; for example, line up the F directly under the A. A plain border of ten stitches separating each letter on all sides would place the E just to the left of the F in the proper place. The four corners would have larger areas of blank space.

The rug would be approximately 63½ inches by 76 inches. As canvas does not come so wide, you would have to use two 36-inch widths pieced together. This would give you a piece 72 inches wide which would leave approximately 8½ inches of unworked canvas for blocking and hemming. Each piece would be 84 inches long.

ANEMONE

In mythology, Anemone was the name of an exquisite nymph adored by Zephyr, god of the west wind. Flora, the Roman goddess of flowers, was jealous of Anemone's beauty, and so banished her from the court, finally transforming her into the exquisitely breezy flower that bears her name.

Numerous varieties of Anemones bloom radiantly in shades of pink, white, purple, sky blue, cream, red and yellow.

The roots when pounded and boiled and applied to an injury were often used to soothe the wounds of North American Indians.

The following colors were used:

B	TRUE RED	P R-10
	TRUE RED	C-M R-10
A	FUCHSIA	P 644
	DAZZLE	C-M 645
■	PURPLE CLARET	P 221
	PURPLE CLARET	C-M 221
·	BRILLIANT GREEN	P 559
	BRILLIANT GREEN	C-M 559
D	SPRING APPLE GREEN	P G-64
	SPRING APPLE GREEN	C-M G-64
C	WHITE	P 001
	WHITE	C-M 005
▦	PUMPKIN SEED	P Y-40
	PUMPKIN SEED	C-M 975
◩	BLACK	P 050
	BLACK	C-M 050

Geometric Pattern

YELLOW	P 450
YELLOW	C-M 450

Overall Background

WHITE	P 001
WHITE	C-M 005

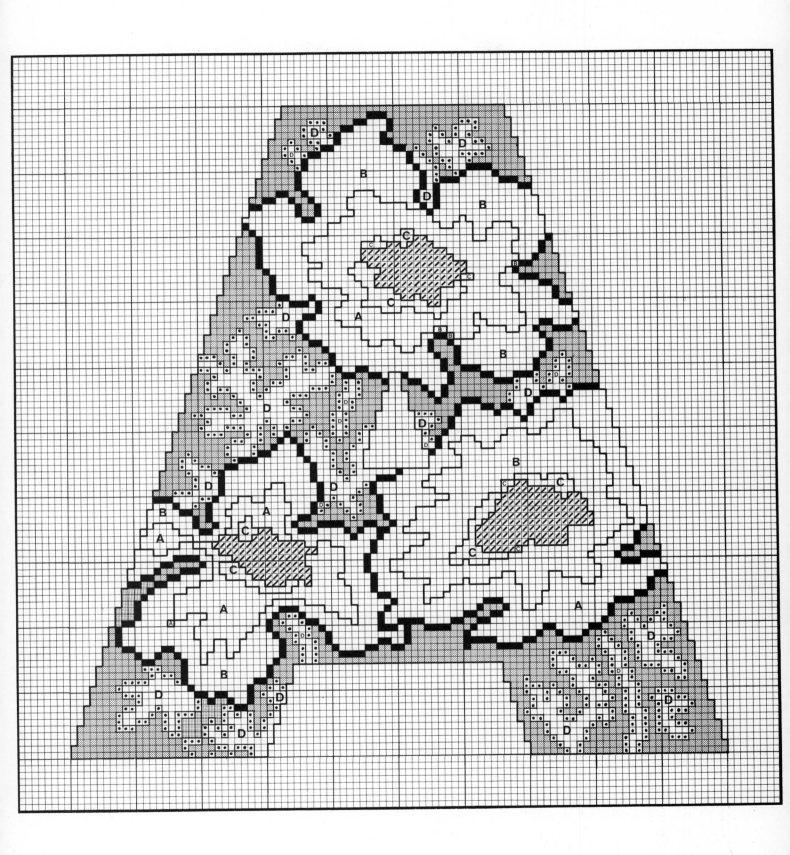

BEET

Beetroots are an ancient vegetable originally cultivated for their colorful young leaves. Ancient Romans discovered their edibly sweet roots. Ever since they have been widely used in cooking, lending their solid texture and hearty sweet flavor.

Beets thrive best in cool climates and are frequently used in Northern European and North American cuisine. The Russians contributed borscht to the New World palate, a hearty beet soup with as many varieties as there are Russians. Americans claim credit for the sweet and sour recipe for Harvard beets and, not to be omitted from the competition, Yale beets are enjoyed by those wanting a sweeter version of this classic recipe.

The expression "beet red" is descriptive of most beets, but they also grow in yellow or white.

The following colors were used:

■	PURPLE CLARET	P 221
	PURPLE CLARET	C-M 221
E	FUCHSIA	P 644
	DAZZLE	C-M 645
C	CERISE	P 649
	CERISE	C-M 827
G	LIGHT APPLE GREEN	P G-74
	LIGHT APPLE GREEN	C-M G-74
B	APPLE GREEN	P 569
	APPLE GREEN	C-M 569
·	DARK GREEN	P 524
	DARK GREEN	C-M 524
▦	SUMMER BLUE	P 743
	SUMMER BLUE	C-M 756

Geometric Pattern

MEXICAN PINK	P 828
MEXICAN PINK	C-M 828

Overall Background

WHITE	P 001
WHITE	C-M 005

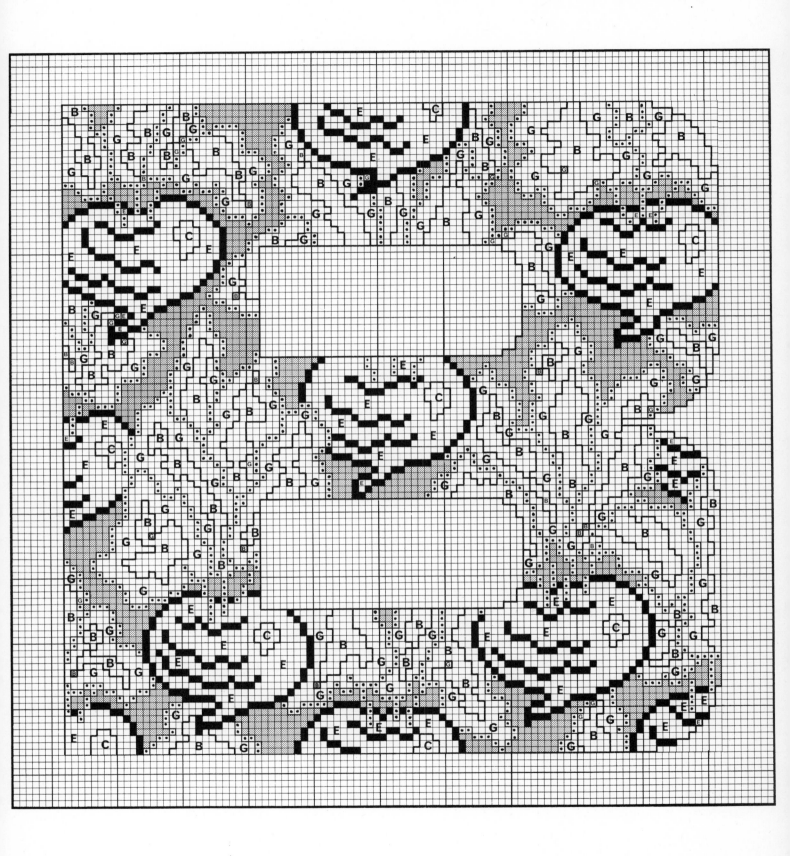

CHERRY

With the warmth of summer, numerous species of birds will quickly pluck the juiciest cherries from the trees in a winning race between humans and birds for the harvest.

Cherry trees bloom in early spring and the blossoms are incredibly lovely in their pink and white breathtaking beauty. The fruit colors are dark red to black, purplish-black, bright red, yellow and pink.

The following colors were used:

■	CRANBERRY	P 240
	CRANBERRY	C-M 240
A	TRUE RED	P R-10
	TRUE RED	C-M R-10
⊠	MIDNIGHT GREEN	P 506
	MIDNIGHT GREEN	C-M 506
·	BRILLIANT GREEN	P 559
	BRILLIANT GREEN	C-M 559
B	SEAWEED	P 574
	SEAWEED	C-M 574
▦	LIGHT YELLOW	P 452
	LIGHT YELLOW	C-M 452
C	WHITE	P 001
	WHITE	C-M 005

Geometric Pattern

CORNFLOWER BLUE	P 731
CORNFLOWER BLUE	C-M 731

Overall Background

WHITE	P 001
WHITE	C-M 005

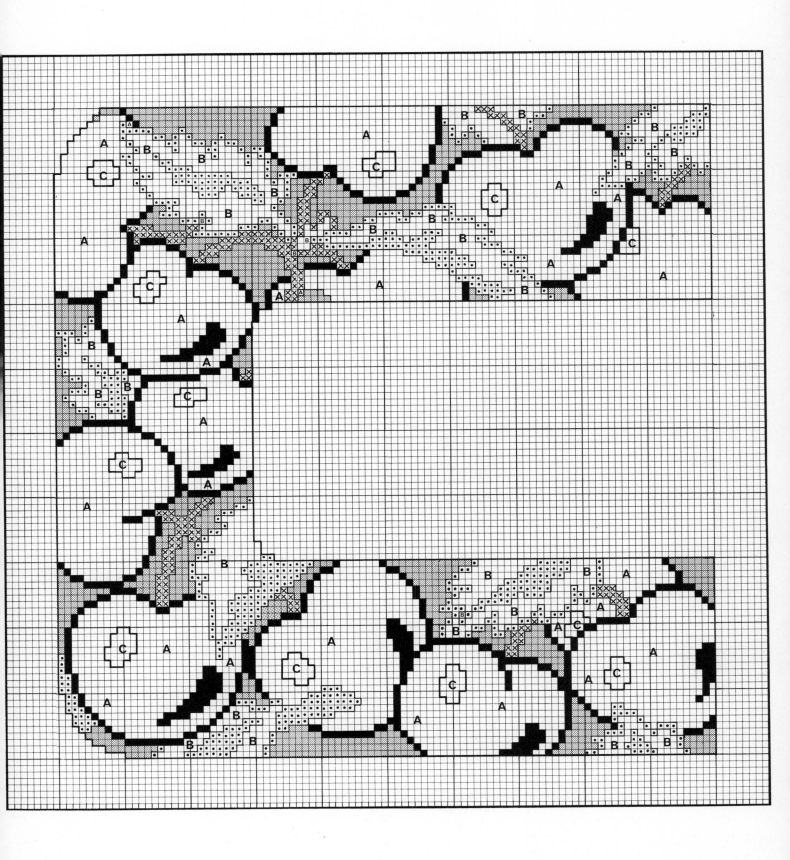

DAFFODIL

In the language of flowers, daffodil means chivalry. It is the large, trumpet-shaped flower which belongs to the Narcissus family. We all know the legend of the vain youth Narcissus, who was loved by all the fair young maidens but who loved only his own watery reflection. He died longing for his elusive image. The nymphs whom he had scorned caused a lovely flower to grow where his body had fallen and gave it his name.

Spring gardens are incomplete without joyous bursts of sun-bright daffodils planted in informal groupings of cream, yellow, white and gold to dazzle the winter weary eye.

The following colors were used:

A	CARROT	P 965
	CARROT	C-M 965
■	PUMPKIN SEED	P Y-40
	PUMPKIN SEED	C-M 975
□	LIGHT YELLOW	P 452
	LIGHT YELLOW	C-M 452
⊠	BRILLIANT GREEN	P 559
	BRILLIANT GREEN	C-M 559
⊡	SPRING APPLE GREEN	P G-64
	SPRING APPLE GREEN	C-M G-64
▦	LIGHT APPLE GREEN	P G-74
	LIGHT APPLE GREEN	C-M G-74

Geometric Pattern

CARROT	P 965
CARROT	C-M 965

Overall Background

WHITE	P 001
WHITE	C-M 005

EGGPLANT

The eggplant (or aubergine) has been cultivated for its fleshy fruit and cooked as a vegetable since the Arabs were bold enough to try it in the fourth century.

A rich and splendid eggplant dish is moussaka, originally from Turkey and adopted by the Greeks, and the most delicious route to a vegetarian's palate is Eggplant Parmigiana, baked until bubbly, its essence of cheese, eggplant and herbs fragrant and savory.

Although the purple eggplant is the best-known variety, other eggplants range in color from green, white or cream to a mottled purple.

The following colors were used:

⊠	INDIGO	P 640
	INDIGO	C-M 640
Ⓐ	BRIGHT PURPLE	P 642
	BRIGHT PURPLE	C-M 642
Ⓑ	LILAC	P 652
	LILAC	C-M 652
■	SPRING APPLE GREEN	P G-64
	SPRING APPLE GREEN	C-M G-64
Ⓒ	LIGHT APPLE GREEN	P G-74
	LIGHT APPLE GREEN	C-M G-74
▨	YELLOW	P 450
	YELLOW	C-M 450

Geometric Pattern

LIGHT MEDIUM BLUE	P 754
LIGHT MEDIUM BLUE	C-M 754

Overall Background

WHITE	P 001
WHITE	C-M 005

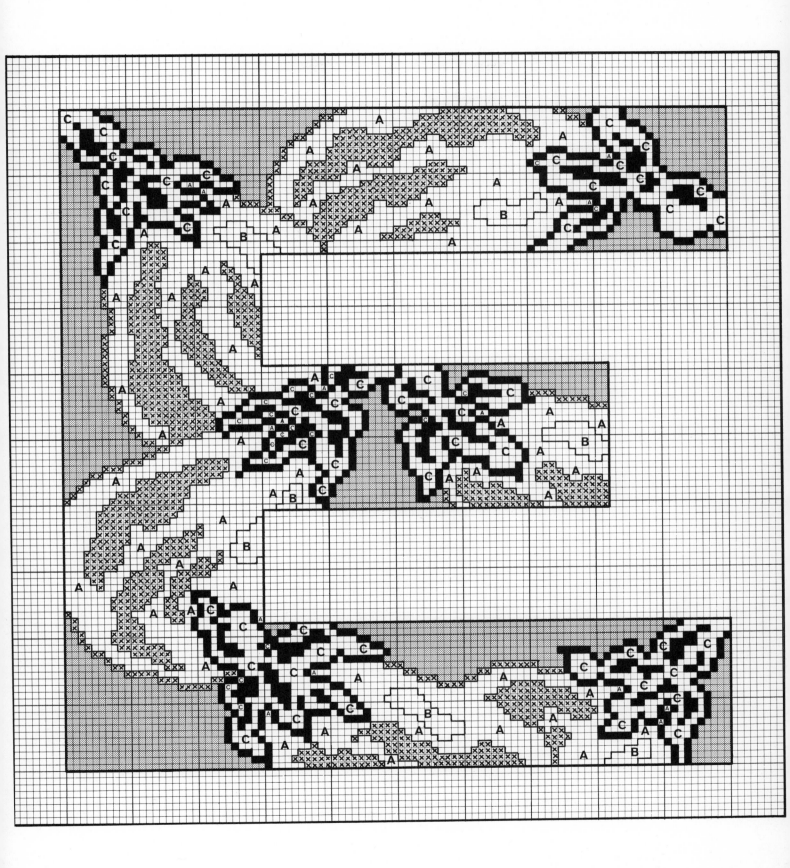

FUCHSIA

The fuchsia of the evening primrose family is native to Central and South America and New Zealand and secretly thrives in their damp and shady mountainous regions and hushed forest interiors.

The exquisite pendulous blossoms, sometimes called ladies' eardrops, droop like silken tassels in colors of pink and red, all pink, crimson and white, salmon-orange, all white, lavender, blue and pink, purple and red.

They are a familiar warm weather sight hanging languidly in baskets on cool, shady verandahs or as garden plants preferring the sunless side of the summer garden.

The following colors were used:

E	FUCHSIA	P 644
	DAZZLE	C-M 645
■	CERISE	P 649
	CERISE	C-M 827
✕	MEXICAN PINK	P 828
	MEXICAN PINK	C-M 828
G	TRUE RED	P R-10
	TRUE RED	C-M R-10
◤	BRILLIANT GREEN	P 559
	BRILLIANT GREEN	C-M 559
▦	SPRING APPLE GREEN	P G-64
	SPRING APPLE GREEN	C-M G-64
·	LIGHT APPLE GREEN	P G-74
	LIGHT APPLE GREEN	C-M G-74

Geometric Pattern

LIGHT APPLE GREEN	P G-74
LIGHT APPLE GREEN	C-M G-74

Overall Background

WHITE	P 001
WHITE	C-M 005

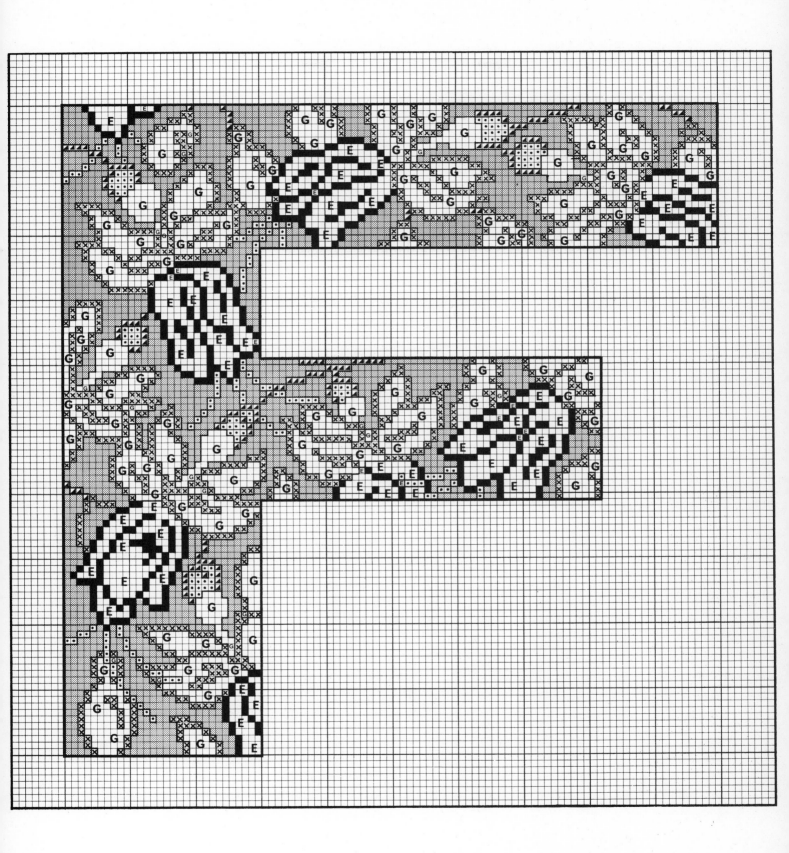

GRAPE

Grapes are enjoyed both fresh and dried; they have been fermented for wine and their vines have been valued for their ornamental shade on garden trellises and arbors since biblical times.

With their heart-shaped leaves, grapes form graceful clusters offering us infinite varieties of sweet succulence from wines and raisins to juices and jellies.

Their colors range from pink, red and reddish-purple, black purple, yellow-green, pale and dull green, to greenish-white.

The following colors were used:

■	BRIGHT PURPLE	P 642
	BRIGHT PURPLE	C-M 642
A	LIGHT PURPLE	P 650
	LIGHT PURPLE	C-M 650
·	SUMMER BLUE	P 743
	SUMMER BLUE	C-M 756
×	DARK GREEN	P 524
	DARK GREEN	C-M 524
G	SPRING APPLE GREEN	P G-64
	SPRING APPLE GREEN	C-M G-64
▦	LIGHT APPLE GREEN	P G-74
	LIGHT APPLE GREEN	C-M G-74
+	BARK BROWN	P 131
	NOT AVAILABLE IN C-M	

Geometric Pattern

YELLOW	P 450
YELLOW	C-M 450

Overall Background

WHITE	P 001
WHITE	C-M 005

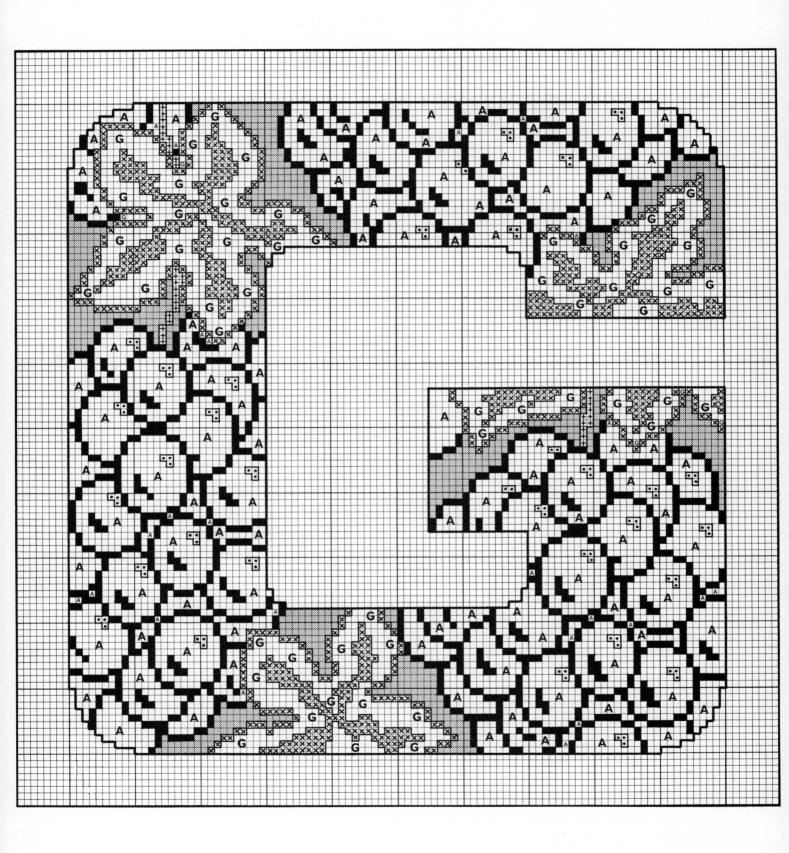

HYACINTH

According to Greek legend, the great beauty of Hyacinthus attracted the love of both Apollo and Zephyr, who was god of the west wind. During a discus-throwing game between Apollo and Hyacinthus, Zephyr, in a jealous rage, blew the discus against the head of Hyacinthus, thus causing a mortal wound. Apollo held him in his arms and tried to stanch the blood, but to no avail. From the bloodstained ground, Apollo created the beautiful bell-like blossoms of the hyacinth.

The hyacinth is a bulb easily grown indoors, bringing the promise of spring with its sweetly fragrant smell and exquisite colors in a delightful range of salmon-pink, pink to red, pale blue to dark blue and purple, white and yellow.

The following colors were used:

⊡	CRANBERRY	P 240
	CRANBERRY	C-M 240
■	CERISE	P 649
	CERISE	C-M 827
☐	MEXICAN PINK	P 828
	MEXICAN PINK	C-M 828
⊠	DARK GREEN	P 524
	DARK GREEN	C-M 524
Ⓓ	SPRING APPLE GREEN	P G-64
	SPRING APPLE GREEN	C-M G-64
Ⓒ	LIGHT APPLE GREEN	P G-74
	LIGHT APPLE GREEN	C-M G-74
▦	TURQUOISE	P 748
	TURQUOISE	C-M 748

Geometric Pattern

LIGHT AQUA	P 728
LIGHT AQUA	C-M 728

Overall Background

WHITE	P 001
WHITE	C-M 005

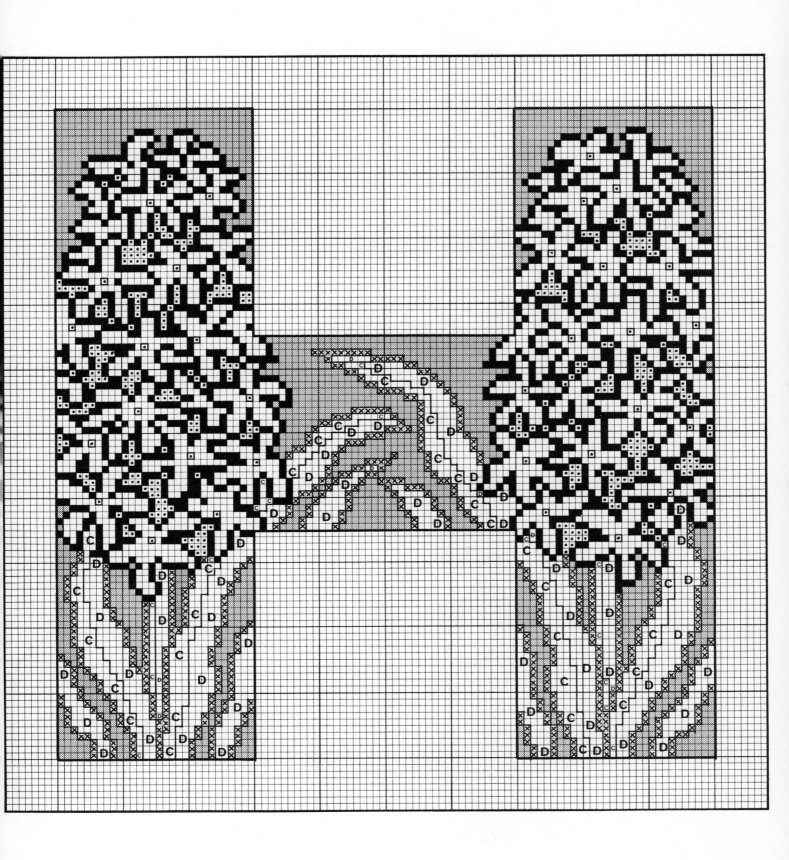

IRIS

The spectacular iris is aptly named after the Greek goddess of the rainbow for it blooms in iridescent and striking hues representing every color in the spectrum. Sometimes called flags, they include more than 200 wild species and many thousands of hybrids.

Though each individual variety is short-lived (one to three weeks), the prolific species of iris offer a long and orderly procession of colorful bloomers from early spring into summer's intense heat, gloriously adapting to changes in the season's temperature. Their showy floral splendor creates dramatic reflections when they are planted near water; artists have delighted in reproducing the line, form and color of iris. Its colors range from tones of rose, white with a contrasting color, lavender, violet, purple, brown, tan, to cream and yellow.

The following colors were used:

■	DARK BLUE	P 721
	DARK BLUE	C-M 740
B	GYPSY BLUE	P 611
	GYPSY BLUE	C-M 611
⊡	MEDIUM BLUE	P 752
	MEDIUM BLUE	C-M 752
A	SUMMER BLUE	P 743
	SUMMER BLUE	C-M 756
C	LIGHT YELLOW	P 452
	LIGHT YELLOW	C-M 452
⊠	DARK GREEN	P 524
	DARK GREEN	C-M 524
⊞	APPLE GREEN	P 569
	APPLE GREEN	C-M 569
D	LIGHT APPLE GREEN	P G-74
	LIGHT APPLE GREEN	C-M G-74
▦	PUMPKIN SEED	P Y- 40
	PUMPKIN SEED	C-M 975

Geometric Pattern

LILAC	P 652
LILAC	C-M 652

Overall Background

WHITE	P 001
WHITE	C-M 005

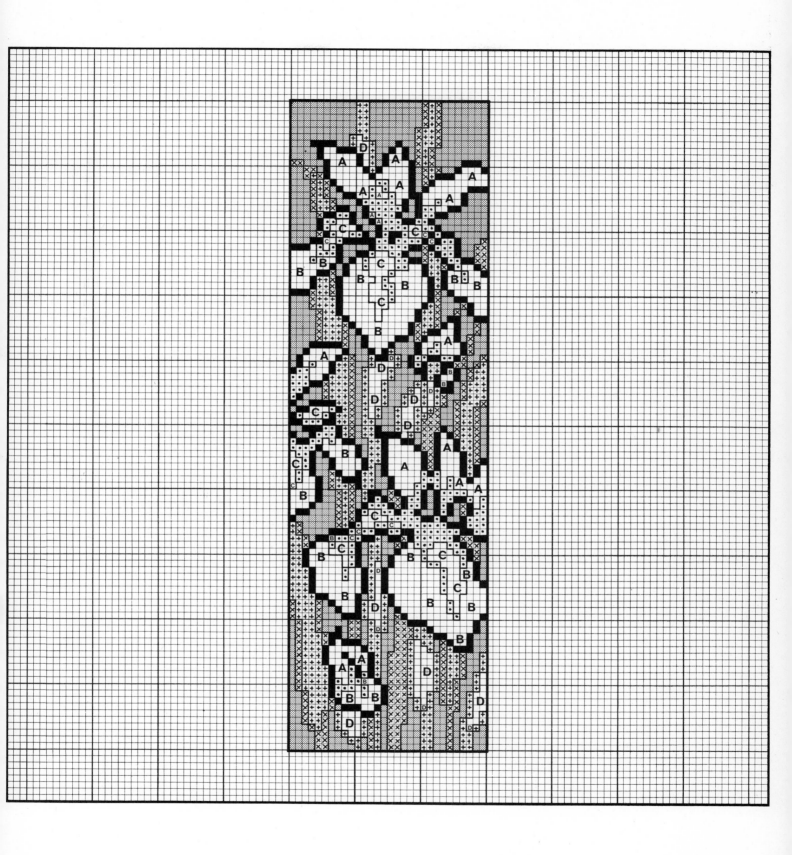

JASMINE

The jasmine, the climbing member of the olive family, claims its origins from the warmer regions of the Old World. Its delicately pointed petals emit a wondrous scent reminiscent of langorous tropical evenings.

The Chinese combine two species of jasmine for tea, and Hawaiians twist its lovely blossoms into fragrant leis.

Its colors are pink to rose, white and yellow.

The following colors were used:

■	PUMPKIN SEED PUMPKIN SEED	P Y-40 C-M 975
Ⓐ	YELLOW YELLOW	P 450 C-M 450
☒	HUNTER GREEN HUNTER GREEN	P 520 C-M 520
⊡	GREEN GIANT GREEN GIANT	P 555 C-M 555
▦	CERISE CERISE	P 649 C-M 827

Geometric Pattern

MEXICAN PINK   P 828
MEXICAN PINK   C-M 828

Overall Background

WHITE   P 001
WHITE   C-M 005

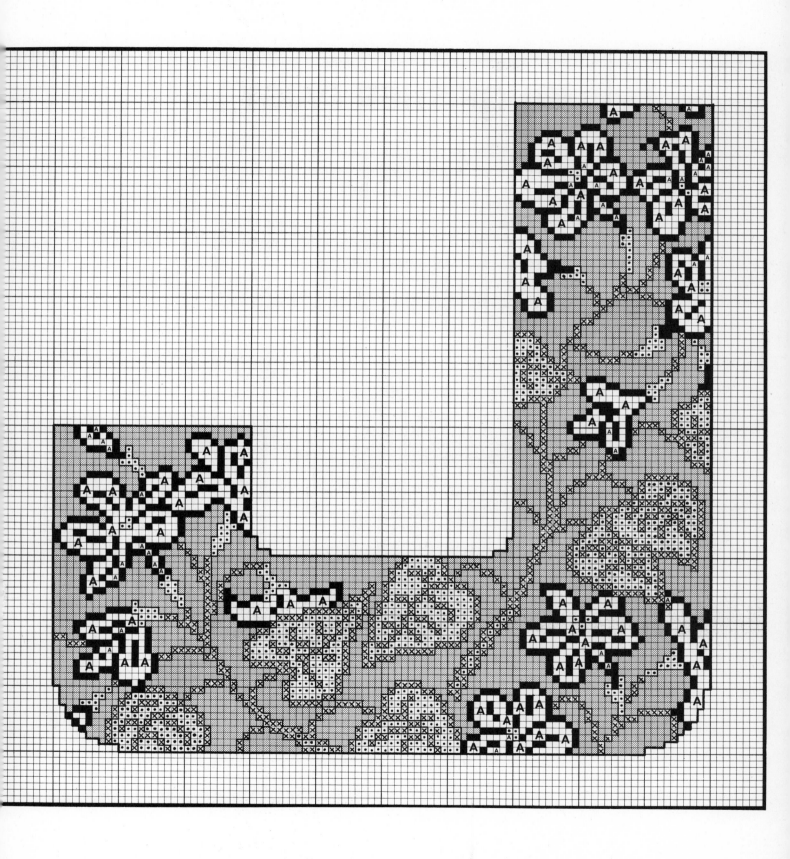

98

KINGFISHER DAISY

The kingfisher daisy is a lovely delicate annual from South Africa with bright cornflower blue petals around a yellow center. The word daisy comes from the ancient Anglo-Saxon word meaning "day's eye," so aptly symbolizing its upturned bright and cheerful face.

It grows abundantly and generously, disliking great amounts of heat but welcoming the sun. Its nectar is secreted in the base of the flower and carefully protected from rain and dew and the visits of undesirable insects.

The following colors were used:

CORNFLOWER BLUE   P 731
CORNFLOWER BLUE   C-M 731

MISTY BLUE   P 741
MISTY BLUE   C-M 741

PUMPKIN SEED   P Y-40
PUMPKIN SEED   C-M 975

YELLOW   P 450
YELLOW   C-M 450

DARK ORANGE   P 958
DARK ORANGE   C-M 958

APPLE GREEN   P 569
APPLE GREEN   C-M 569

LIGHT APPLE GREEN   P G-74
LIGHT APPLE GREEN   C-M G-74

Geometric Pattern

LIGHT ORANGE   P 970
LIGHT ORANGE   C-M 970

Overall Background

WHITE   P 001
WHITE   C-M 005

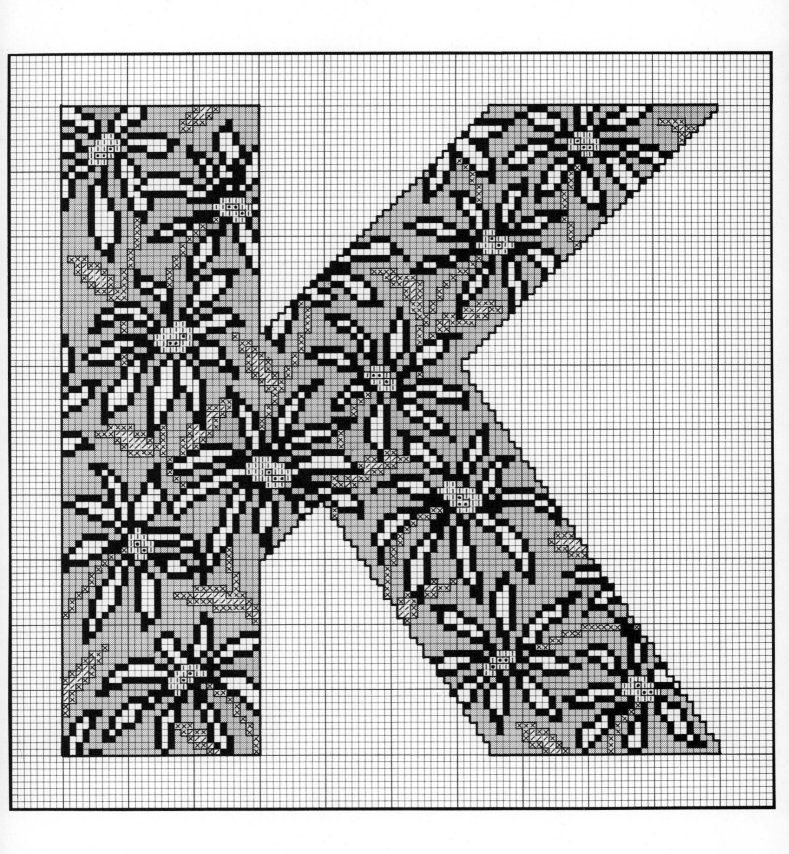

LEEK

The most majestic of green onions is the leek, which has been adopted by Welshmen as their national emblem. Ironically, it had been derided for centuries because of its weedlike availability. Its versatility as a delicious vegetable has been ignored, and it is merely used for flavoring soups and stews. The leek, a winter vegetable, is a major ingredient of the classic summer soup vichyssoise, a rich, creamy culinary triumph.

American Indian tribes crushed the leek's bulbs and used the juice to relieve the pain of insect stings, and the Menominee tribe christened a region rich in the strong smelling wild leeks "shika'ko," or "skunk place." This is now Chicago, where the smells of the stockyards and other modern pollutants have long since buried that of the mildly odorous leek.

The following colors were used:

■	HUNTER GREEN	P 520
	HUNTER GREEN	C-M 520
⊡	GREEN GIANT	P 555
	GREEN GIANT	C-M 555
⊘	LIGHT APPLE GREEN	P G-74
	LIGHT APPLE GREEN	C-M G-74
⊠	TOBACCO	P 145
	TOBACCO	C-M 145
▨	PUMPKIN SEED	P Y-40
	PUMPKIN SEED	C-M 975
☐	WHITE	P 001
	WHITE	C-M 005

Geometric Pattern

YELLOW	P 450
YELLOW	C-M 450

Overall Background

WHITE	P 001
WHITE	C-M 005

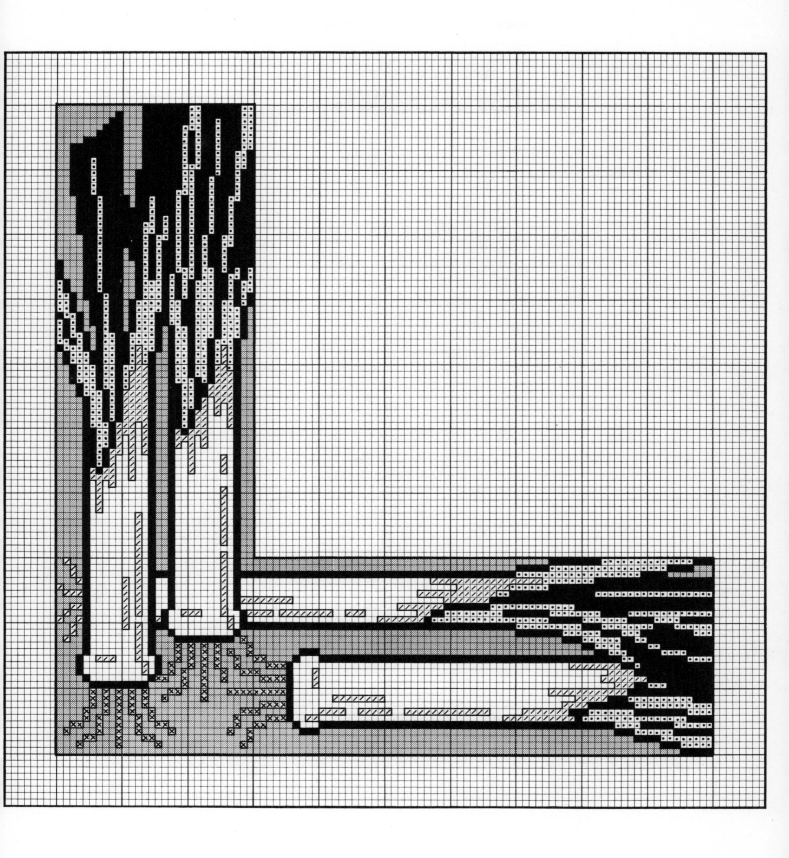

MUSHROOMS

Mushrooms are neither vegetable nor fruit but fungi and parasitic. They depend on decaying vegetation and animal matter for growth and nourishment, and a single mushroom yields millions of spores, which are spread by the wind for its reproduction. A dieter's delight, mushrooms are higher in minerals than most vegetables and very low in calories, and there are unlimited culinary possibilities for mushrooms hot or cold.

Of the many poisonous species of mushrooms, the deadliest is aptly named Destroying Angel, which is the brilliant red that Jack has shown in the design. The cultivated mushroom that we enjoy is creamy white, beige or rich brown.

The following colors were used:

☑	MEDIUM GREEN	P 510
	MEDIUM GREEN	C-M 510
D	LIGHT APPLE GREEN	P G-74
	LIGHT APPLE GREEN	C-M G-74
+	CRANBERRY	P 240
	CRANBERRY	C-M 240
−	DARK ORANGE	P 958
	DARK ORANGE	C-M 958
◉	BURNT ORANGE	P 960
	BURNT ORANGE	C-M 960
·	PUMPKIN SEED	P Y-40
	PUMPKIN SEED	C-M 975
G	CANARY YELLOW	P Y-44
	CANARY YELLOW	C-M 457
A	LIGHT YELLOW	P 452
	LIGHT YELLOW	C-M 452
⊐	WOOD BROWN	P 217
	WOOD BROWN	C-M 217
C	COPPERTONE	P 410
	COPPERTONE	C-M 410
B	PALE RUST	P 423
	PALE RUST	C-M 423

F	PALE PINK	P 831
	PALE PINK	C-M 831
■	DEEP BROWN	P 110
	DEEP BROWN	C-M 114
◩	TOBACCO	P 145
	TOBACCO	C-M 145
E	BEIGE	P 492
	BEIGE	C-M 492
⊠	BARK BROWN	P 131
	NOT AVAILABLE IN C-M	
▦	LILAC	P 652
	LILAC	C-M 652
⊡	WHITE	P 001
	WHITE	C-M 005

Geometric Pattern

LIGHT APPLE GREEN	P G-74
LIGHT APPLE GREEN	C-M G-74

Overall Background

WHITE	P 001
WHITE	C-M 005

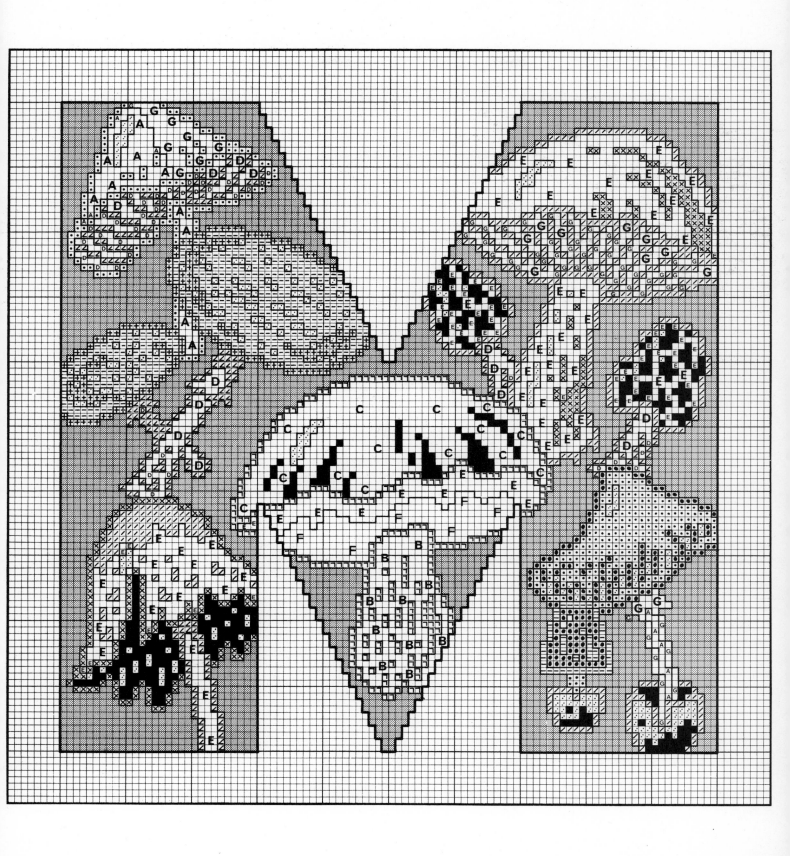

NASTURTIUM

The scientific name for nasturtium is *Tropaeolum*. Native to South America, the nasturtium has trailing vines and low plants that bloom in summer in brilliant hues, from pure yellow to rich orange to red. They thrive in the hot summer sun but are willing to bloom until the frost.

Nasturtiums are used both for beauty and food, sometimes both at the same time, as even the brilliant flowers are edible and can be used to make designs on salads, vegetables and meats.

The slightly bitter stems and leaves of the nasturtium plant, readily used in salads and pickling, resemble the watercress—or *Nasturtium officionale*—which is how the nasturtium got its name.

The following colors were used:

D	CRANBERRY	P 240
	CRANBERRY	C-M 240
■	DARK ORANGE	P 958
	DARK ORANGE	C-M 958
C	BURNT ORANGE	P 960
	BURNT ORANGE	C-M 960
◪	PUMPKIN SEED	P Y-40
	PUMPKIN SEED	C-M 975
E	LIGHT YELLOW	P 452
	LIGHT YELLOW	C-M 452
−	BRILLIANT GREEN	P 559
	BRILLIANT GREEN	C-M 559
⊠	APPLE GREEN	P 569
	APPLE GREEN	C-M 569
⊡	SEAWEED	P 574
	SEAWEED	C-M 574
⊙	LIGHT APPLE GREEN	P G-74
	LIGHT APPLE GREEN	C-M G-74
▦	CORNFLOWER BLUE	P 731
	CORNFLOWER BLUE	C-M 731

Geometric Pattern

MISTY BLUE	P 741
MISTY BLUE	C-M 741

Overall Background

WHITE	P 001
WHITE	C-M 005

ONION

The onion, with its numerous layers of paper-thin skin, was treasured in antiquity as a symbol of eternity. Used as a food since ancient times, it is a member of the lily family and has been grown since early recorded history. The common white onion is strong and lusty and is used casually in stews and casseroles and frying. The grand and beautiful Spanish and Italian onions are sweetly mild enough to be eaten raw on freshly buttered bread or with a sizzling hamburger, but don't plan on a close romantic encounter too soon after eating them.

Onion colors are white, purple-red or shades of yellow-gold.

The following colors were used:

◰	EARTH	P 521
	EARTH	C-M 521
⊟	TOPAZ	P 440
	TOPAZ	C-M 440
Ⓐ	LIGHT YELLOW	P 452
	LIGHT YELLOW	C-M 452
■	PURPLE CLARET	P 221
	PURPLE CLARET	C-M 221
◲	FUCHSIA	P 644
	DAZZLE	C-M 645
Ⓑ	CERISE	P 649
	CERISE	C-M 827
⊠	HUNTER GREEN	P 520
	HUNTER GREEN	C-M 520
⊡	SPRING APPLE GREEN	P G-64
	SPRING APPLE GREEN	C-M G-64
Ⓒ	LIGHT APPLE GREEN	P G-74
	LIGHT APPLE GREEN	C-M G-74
▦	TURQUOISE	P 748
	TURQUOISE	C-M 748
⊡	WHITE	P 001
	WHITE	C-M 005

Geometric Pattern

PALE MAUVE	P 229
PALE MAUVE	C-M 229

Overall Background

WHITE	P 001
WHITE	C-M 005

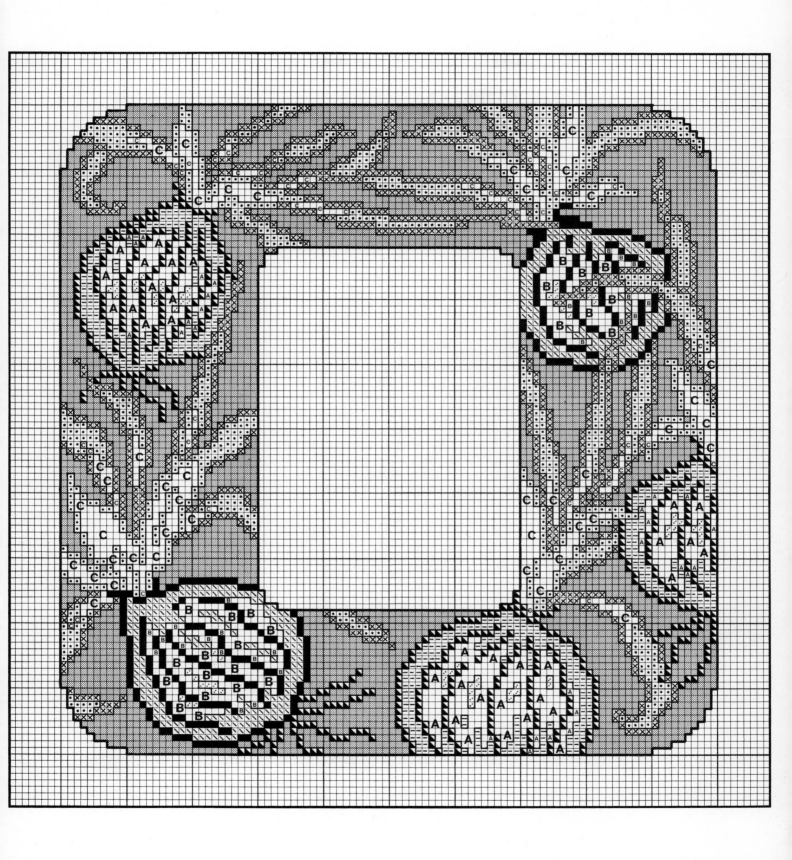

PEPPER

Peppers are divided into two main groups, sweet and hot. Hot peppers, as anyone who has ever tasted Tabasco or cayenne knows, are very hot indeed. If your pet cat eats your favorite plants, a touch of red pepper on the leaves should quickly discourage it. Peppers are eaten both raw and cooked. Although certainly not poisonous, they are members of the Deadly Nightshade family and are also related to tomatoes, eggplants, potatoes and even tobacco. Their colors are dark and light green, bright red, yellow, predominately red with a touch of green and predominately green with a touch of red.

The following colors were used:

◪	CRANBERRY CRANBERRY	P 240 C-M 240
H	TRUE RED TRUE RED	P R-10 C-M R-10
G	DARK ORANGE DARK ORANGE	P 958 C-M 958
×	CARROT CARROT	P 965 C-M 965
S	PUMPKIN SEED PUMPKIN SEED	P Y-40 C-M 975
O	YELLOW YELLOW	P 450 C-M 450
+	HUNTER GREEN HUNTER GREEN	P 520 C-M 520
■	DARK GREEN DARK GREEN	P 524 C-M 524
E	SPRING APPLE GREEN SPRING APPLE GREEN	P G-64 C-M G-64
⊡	GREEN GIANT GREEN GIANT	P 555 C-M 555
J	LIGHT APPLE GREEN LIGHT APPLE GREEN	P G-74 C-M G-74
▦	LIGHT PURPLE LIGHT PURPLE	P 650 C-M 650
A	WHITE WHITE	P 001 C-M 005

Geometric Pattern

SUMMER BLUE SUMMER BLUE	P 743 C-M 756

Overall Background

WHITE WHITE	P 001 C-M 005

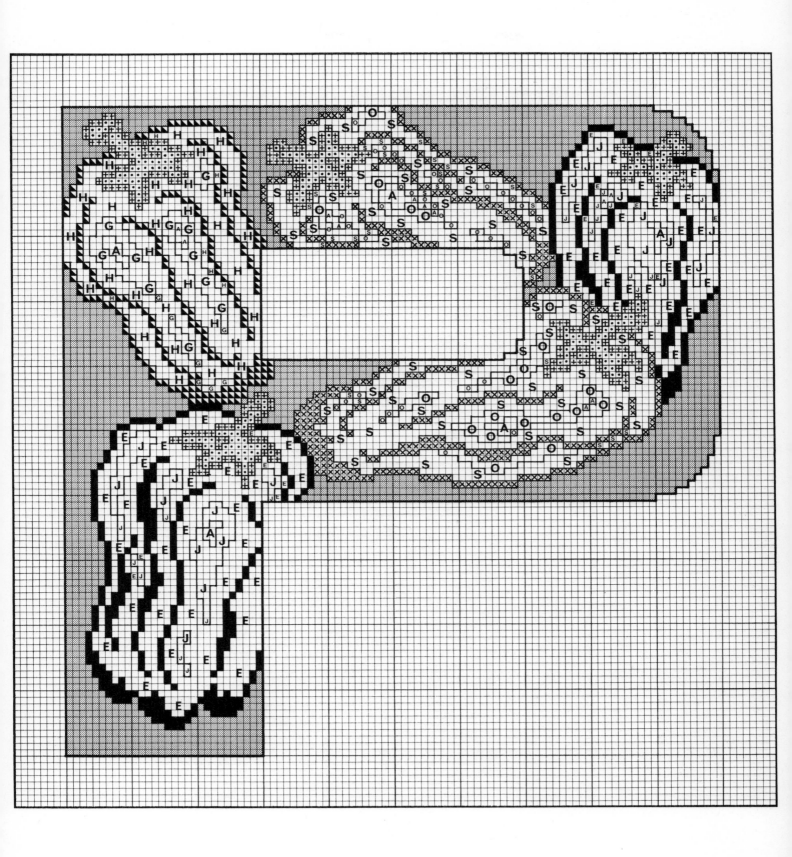

QUEEN ANNE'S LACE

Queen Anne's lace, a lovely, airy, white flower with fernlike leaves, is actually the European wild carrot, although its root is not edible. It spreads quickly and easily and can be found growing wild in fields and by roadsides. Unfortunately, it has become known as a pest to many gardeners who have never paid close attention to the beauty of true wild plants. It is creamy white with a tiny touch of dark purple-red in the center.

The following colors were used:

■	MEDIUM GREEN	P 510
	MEDIUM GREEN	C-M 510
⊠	LIGHT APPLE GREEN	P G-74
	LIGHT APPLE GREEN	C-M G-74
☐	WHITE	P 001
	WHITE	C-M 005
▨	MEXICAN PINK	P 828
	MEXICAN PINK	C-M 828

Geometric Pattern

SUMMER BLUE	P 743
SUMMER BLUE	C-M 756

Overall Background

WHITE	P 001
WHITE	C-M 005

112

RADISH

The radish is a root vegetable; lacking the status of other edible roots, it is treated as an accessory or a condiment. It grows easily and rapidly and can be plucked from the garden to make an appealing and colorful appearance in a summer salad or garnishing a formally designed tray of hors d'oeuvres.

Radishes grow in a variety of shapes (fat and round, elongated), large and small sizes, and several colors (red, white, yellow and black). The young, tender leaves at the top of the small round variety can also be eaten when the radish is served as a *crudité*.

The following colors were used:

■	CRANBERRY	P 240
	CRANBERRY	C-M 240
E	TRUE RED	P R-10
	TRUE RED	C-M R-10
⊡	PALE MAUVE	P 229
	PALE MAUVE	C-M 229
⊠	BRILLIANT GREEN	P 559
	BRILLIANT GREEN	C-M 559
⊟	SEAWEED	P 574
	SEAWEED	C-M 574
▦	YELLOW	P 450
	YELLOW	C-M 450
O	WHITE	P 001
	WHITE	C-M 005

Geometric Pattern

LIGHT APPLE GREEN	P G-74
LIGHT APPLE GREEN	C-M G-74

Overall Background

WHITE	P 001
WHITE	C-M 005

STRING BEANS

String beans are also called snap beans, green beans and wax beans and are at their succulent best when the pods are young and thin and snap crisply when broken.

Green beans were an important contribution to Europe from the New World. When left to mature on the vine, the beans can be dried for storage. Dried beans were exported to Europe where they were used with meat for rich casseroles.

The name "string bean" no longer really applies because modern string beans are stringless; if you find beans with strings they are not good quality. String beans are either green or yellow.

The following colors were used:

■	BRILLIANT GREEN	P 559
	BRILLIANT GREEN	C-M 559
□	SPRING APPLE GREEN	P G-64
	SPRING APPLE GREEN	C-M G-64
⊡	LIGHT APPLE GREEN	P G-74
	LIGHT APPLE GREEN	C-M G-74
▦	LIGHT ORANGE	P 970
	LIGHT ORANGE	C-M 970

Geometric Pattern

MEXICAN PINK	P 828
MEXICAN PINK	C-M 828

Overall Background

WHITE	P 001
WHITE	C-M 005

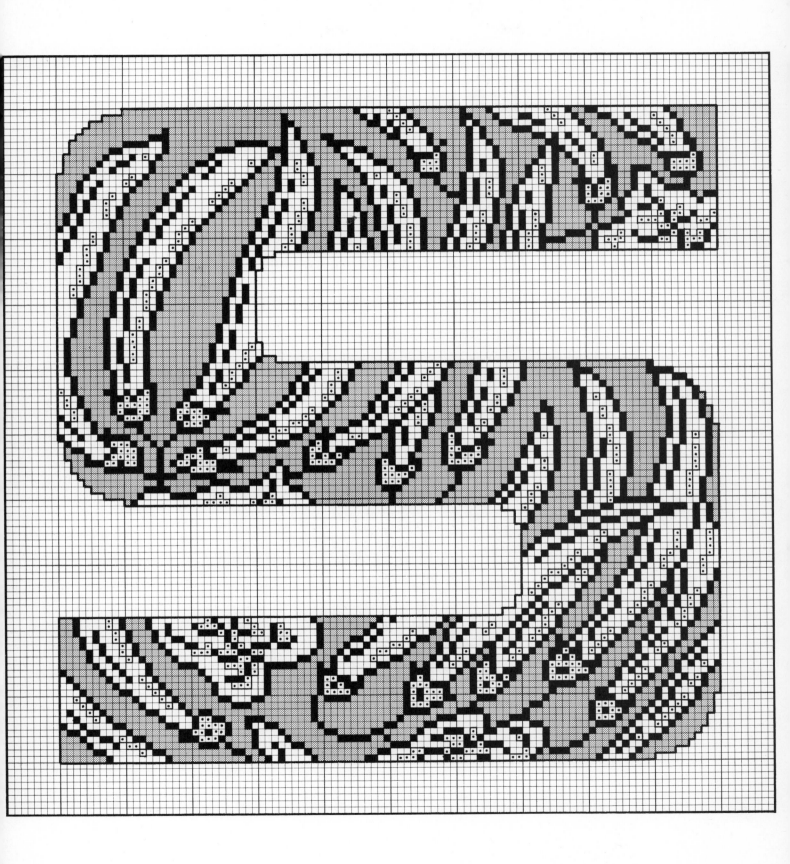

TULIP

Tulip bulbs set into cold autumn soil will yield radiant cup-shaped flowers in early spring, reaffirming Nature's eternal promise of fertility and ornamental splendor.

Gardeners have the pleasurable choice of hundreds of colorful hybrid tulips, which come in every color with the exception of true blue, and those wishing for a touch of the exotic can obtain bulbs for the ragged-edged parrot tulip, tulips with touches of green, multicolored tulips and double tulips with the rich abundance of peony-like flowers.

Tulips were brought to Antwerp, Belgium, in the sixteenth century from Istanbul, but it was in Holland that most of the hybrids we know today were cultivated. In the language of flowers tulips stand for a declaration of love.

The following colors were used:

B	DARK ORANGE	P 958
	DARK ORANGE	C-M 958
■	CARROT	P 965
	CARROT	C-M 965
⋅	CANARY YELLOW	P Y-44
	CANARY YELLOW	C-M 457
A	FOREST GREEN	P 528
	FOREST GREEN	C-M 528
×	BRILLIANT GREEN	P 559
	BRILLIANT GREEN	C-M 559
−	APPLE GREEN	P 569
	APPLE GREEN	C-M 569
▨	LIGHT APPLE GREEN	P G-74
	LIGHT APPLE GREEN	C-M G-74

Geometric Pattern

LIGHT YELLOW	P 452
LIGHT YELLOW	C-M 452

Overall Background

WHITE	P 001
WHITE	C-M 005

UMBRELLA PLANT

Native to the swamps of Africa, the umbrella plant (*Cyperus alternifolius*) has graceful, ribbon-like streamers atop each stalk. These slender leaflets resemble a lovely umbrella. This exotic plant is related to the Egyptian papyrus and grows in the wetlands of Madagascar. There is a dwarf form available.

The following colors were used:

■	HUNTER GREEN	P 520
	HUNTER GREEN	C-M 520
☒	MEDIUM GREEN	P 510
	MEDIUM GREEN	C-M 510
☐	LIGHT APPLE GREEN	P G-74
	LIGHT APPLE GREEN	C-M G-74
▥	MEDIUM ORANGE	P 978
	MEDIUM ORANGE	C-M 978

Background

WHITE	P 001
WHITE	C-M 005

Geometric Pattern

FLESH	P 992
FLESH	C-M 853

VIOLET

Violets are native to all lands within the temperate zone, and their species are many and varied. Some may be found in fields and woods growing wild during spring and early summer. The flowers, though small, have a sweet, distinctive perfume. The most common, of course, is the one which shares its name with the color, but it also blooms in blue, yellow and red as well as creamy-white. Violets are edible and are used for making both tea and candy and as garnishes in salads.

The following colors were used:

■	INDIGO	P 640
	INDIGO	C-M 640
□	BRIGHT PURPLE	P 642
	BRIGHT PURPLE	C-M 642
⊡	LIGHT PURPLE	P 650
	LIGHT PURPLE	C-M 650
⊠	DARK GREEN	P 524
	DARK GREEN	C-M 524
◩	SPRING APPLE GREEN	P G-64
	SPRING APPLE GREEN	C-M G-64
⊞	LIGHT APPLE GREEN	P G-74
	LIGHT APPLE GREEN	C-M G-74
▦	YELLOW	P 450
	YELLOW	C-M 450
A	WHITE	P 001
	WHITE	C-M 005

Geometric Pattern

TURQUOISE	P 748
TURQUOISE	C-M 748

Overall Background

WHITE	P 001
WHITE	C-M 005

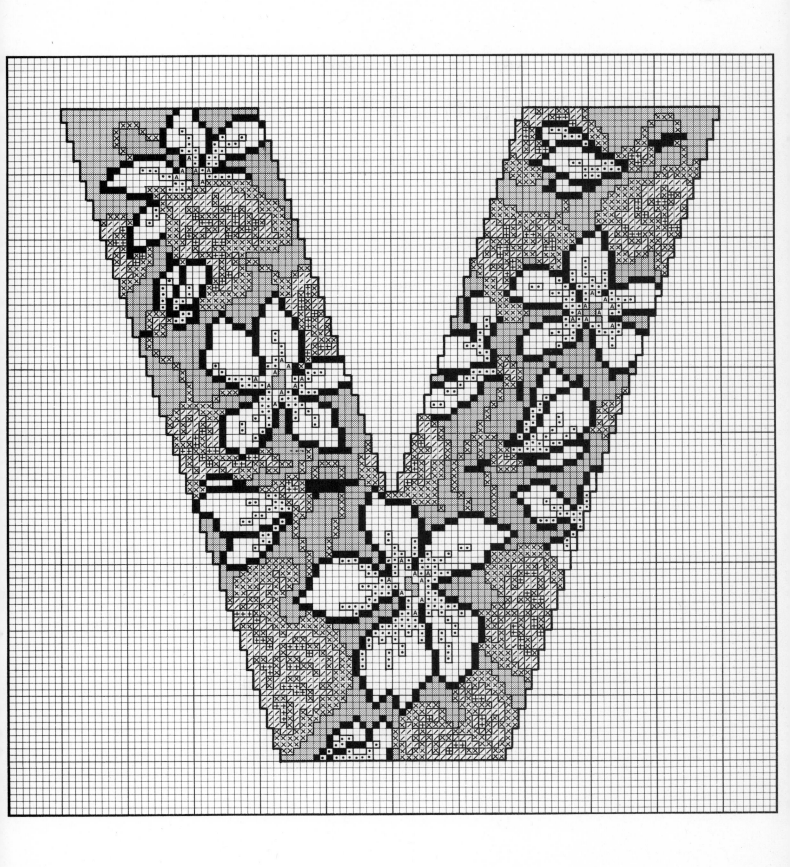

WATER LILY

The waxy texture and sweet, delicate fragrance of the water lily are breathtakingly beautiful. The *Victoria regia*, a giant platter, has been found with leaves large and strong enough to support a child's weight! This type of water lily from the Amazon river boasts leaves 5 to 6 feet in width and 12-inch flowers.

Anchored by an elaborate root system, the water lily floats placidly, forming a protective covering for fish. It conveys an Oriental beauty and quiet order, its leaves resting serenely on the water, its large rosettes of pointed petals curving upward toward their centers. The rosettes are usually a pure opaque white, but they also bloom in reddish-white, yellow and white, light, dark and violet-blue, pink or red and purple-red.

The following colors were used:

■	CERISE CERISE	P 649 C-M 827
⊡	MEXICAN PINK MEXICAN PINK	P 828 C-M 828
◪	TOPAZ TOPAZ	P 440 C-M 440
⊡	YELLOW YELLOW	P 450 C-M 450
⊠	HUNTER GREEN HUNTER GREEN	P 520 C-M 520
S	MEDIUM GREEN MEDIUM GREEN	P 510 C-M 510
⊟	GREEN GIANT GREEN GIANT	P 555 C-M 555
▩	SUMMER BLUE SUMMER BLUE	P 743 C-M 756

Geometric Pattern

	LIGHT PURPLE LIGHT PURPLE	P 650 C-M 650

Overall Background

	WHITE WHITE	P 001 C-M 005

XERANTHEMUM

This plant is commonly called "immortelle" or "everlasting" because its papery blossoms can be cut, hung in bunches in a cool airy place and dried for future use in winter bouquets. With its silvery flower heads and purplish flowers, Xeranthemum bears a close resemblance to the thistle plant.

This eternal plant favors a warm climate and produces flowers in shades of lilac, rose and white.

The following colors were used:

■	MAGENTA	P 623
	MAGENTA	C-M 639
☐	PALE MAUVE	P 229
	PALE MAUVE	C-M 229
☒	HUNTER GREEN	P 520
	HUNTER GREEN	C-M 520
⊡	SEAWEED	P 574
	SEAWEED	C-M 574
▨	PUMPKIN SEED	P Y-40
	PUMPKIN SEED	C-M 975

Geometric Pattern

LIGHT APPLE GREEN	P G-74
LIGHT APPLE GREEN	C-M G-74

Overall Background

WHITE	P 001
WHITE	C-M 005

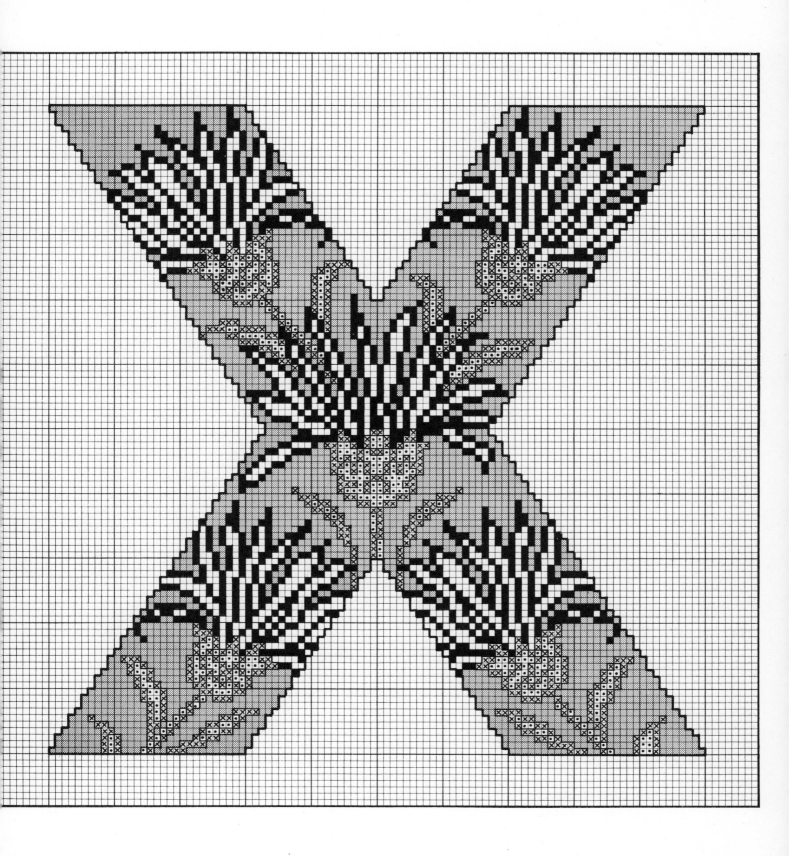

YARROW

The showy yarrow herb has medicinal qualities which are said to have first been discovered by the Greek warrior Achilles when he was studying botany under Cheiron, the centaur. And from this story it has been honored with his name, *Achillea millefolium*.

Although the yarrow plant grows unnoticed in abandoned fields and wasteplaces throughout North America, its medicinal qualities were recognized by the Zuñi Indians of New Mexico to cool burns and heal wounds. Yarrow plants are very independent, requiring neither rich soil nor care. They blossom abundantly in summer, bearing heavy clusters of small white, mustard-yellow or pink flowers.

The following colors were used:

⊡	TOPAZ	P 440
	TOPAZ	C-M 440
⊠	PUMPKIN SEED	P Y-40
	PUMPKIN SEED	C-M 975
☐	LIGHT YELLOW	P 452
	LIGHT YELLOW	C-M 452
■	SPRING APPLE GREEN	P G-64
	SPRING APPLE GREEN	C-M G-64
⊟	LIGHT APPLE GREEN	P G-74
	LIGHT APPLE GREEN	C-M G-74
▨	BRIGHT PURPLE	P 642
	BRIGHT PURPLE	C-M 642

Geometric Pattern

MISTY BLUE	P 741
MISTY BLUE	C-M 741

Overall Background

WHITE	P 001
WHITE	C-M 005

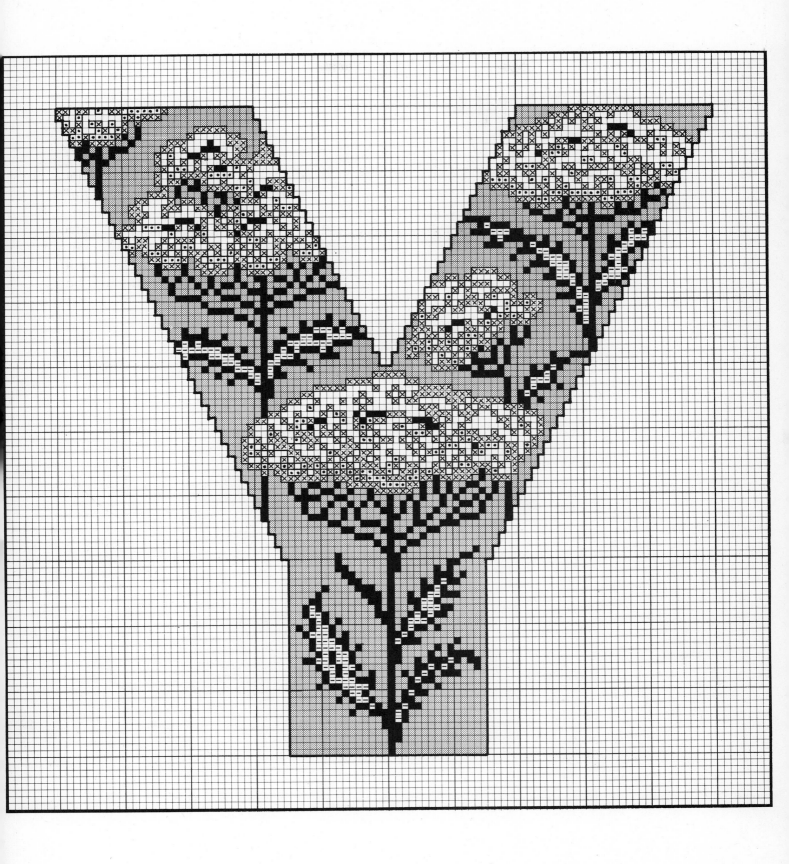

ZINNIA

Zinnia means "Thoughts in Absence." The cultivated plant of today can hardly be recognized as a descendant of the primitive flower that grew wild in the fields and on roadsides. However, even in its simplest state, it is considered handsome. Formerly the blossoms were only scarlet and single, but propagation has doubled them and zinnias now grow in many rich and varied hues, with the exception of blue. It is one of the easiest of garden annuals to grow.

The following colors were used:

⊞	TRUE RED	P R-10
	TRUE RED	C-M R-10
◿	FUCHSIA	P 644
	DAZZLE	C-M 645
◳	BURNT ORANGE	P 960
	BURNT ORANGE	C-M 960
◱	PUMPKIN SEED	P Y-40
	PUMPKIN SEED	C-M 975
⊡	MEXICAN PINK	P 828
	MEXICAN PINK	C-M 828
■	BRILLIANT GREEN	P 559
	BRILLIANT GREEN	C-M 559
⊡	SEAWEED	P 574
	SEAWEED	C-M 574
▦	LIGHT APPLE GREEN	P G-74
	LIGHT APPLE GREEN	C-M G-74

Geometric Pattern

YELLOW	P 450
YELLOW	C-M 450

Overall Background

WHITE	P 001
WHITE	C-M 005

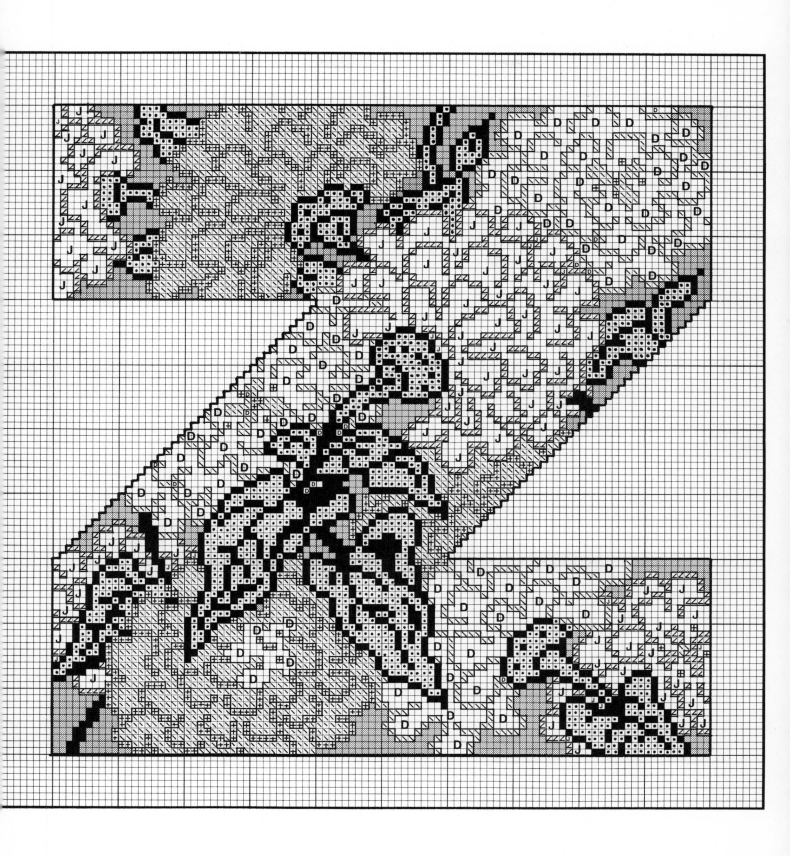

7

Geometric Backgrounds for Letters/Borders

The five geometric background patterns Jack has designed are shown here with the area that would be filled in if you were doing the letter "A" showing the geometric pattern in gray. If you want to use the patterns for another letter or as a background to another project, follow the tracing instructions given on p.138. A pillow in a solid geometric pattern would pair nicely with a pillow featuring a letter with the same geometric pattern in the background. When you see what a stunning effect a geometric pattern in the background of your work can make, you may well be inspired to create additional patterns of your own!

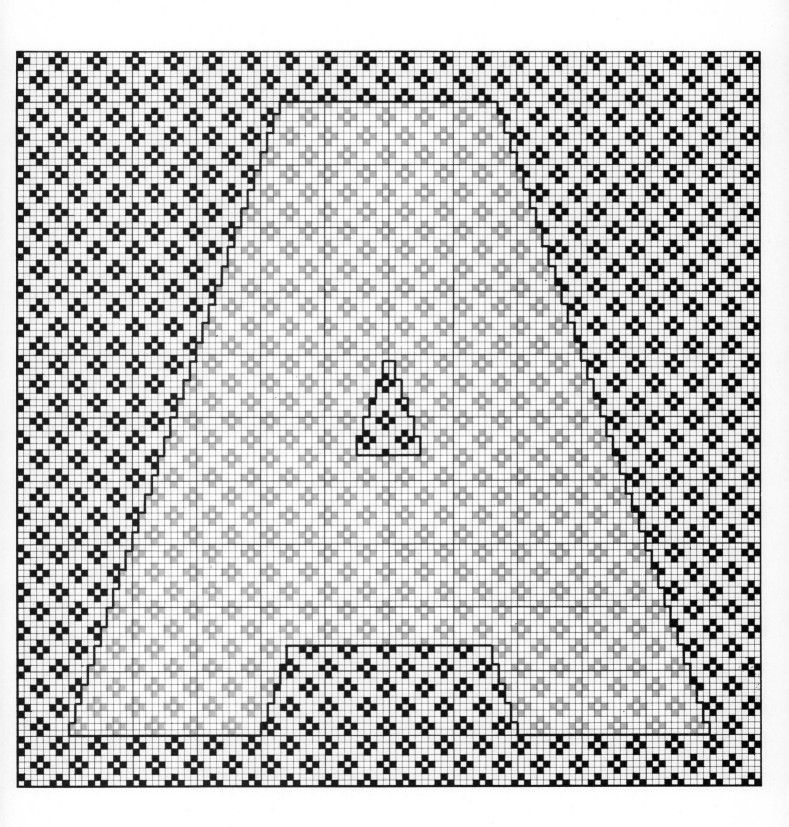

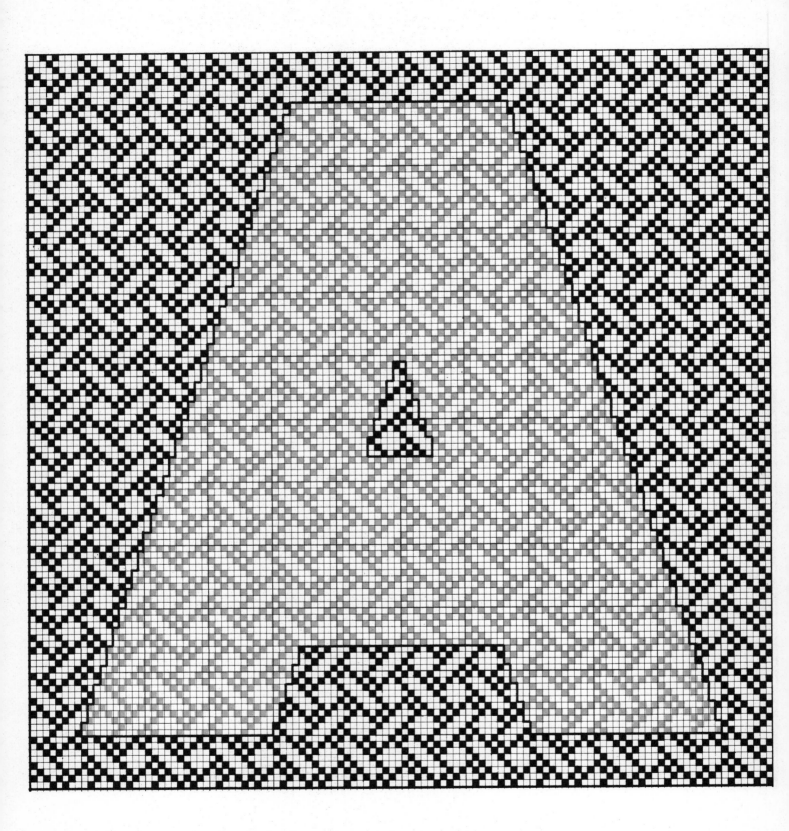

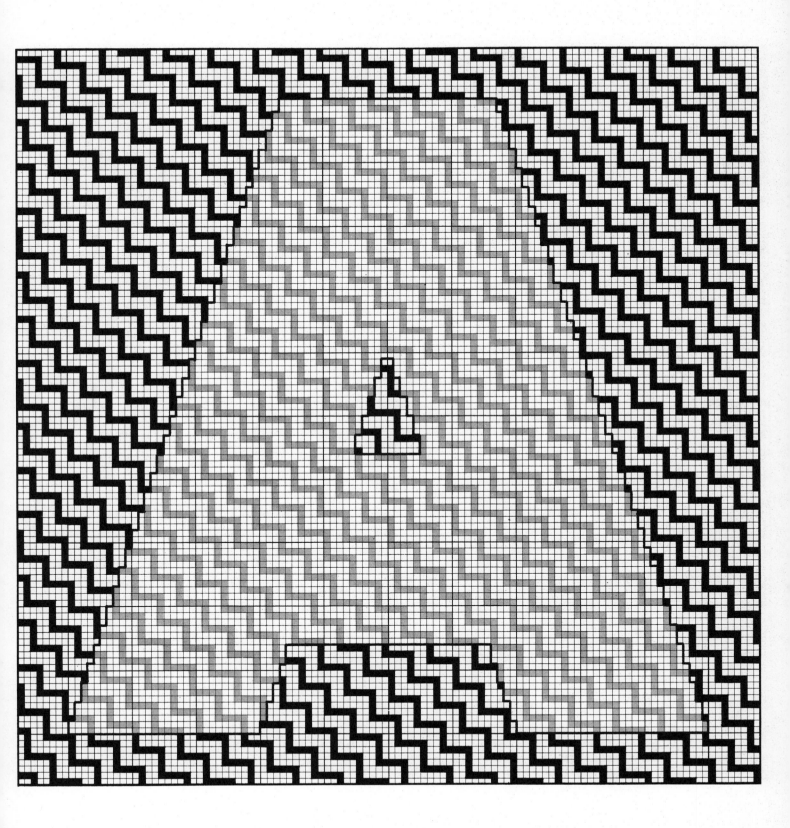

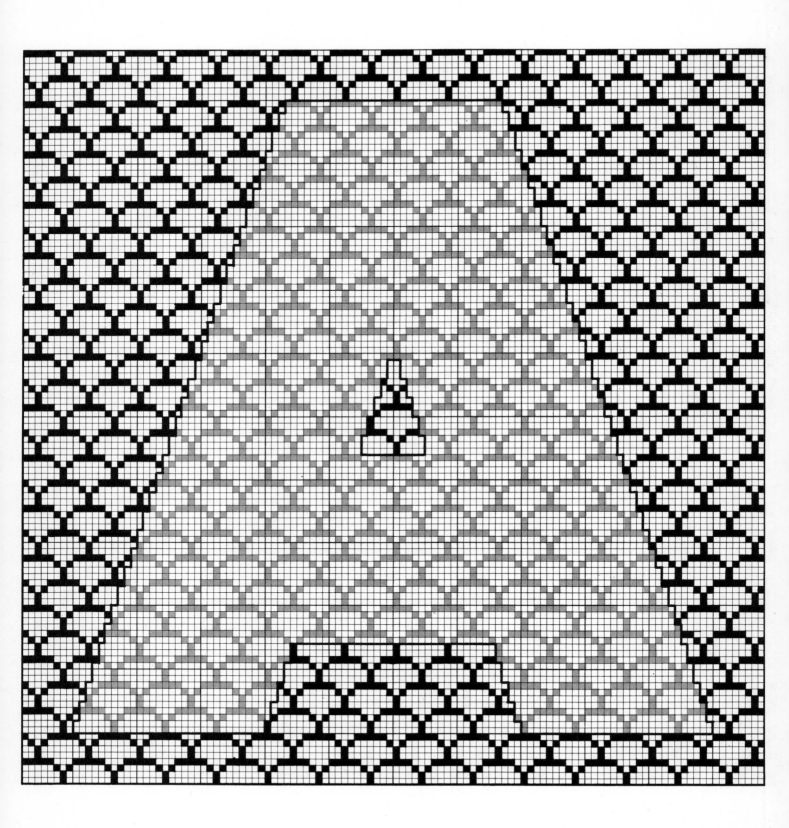

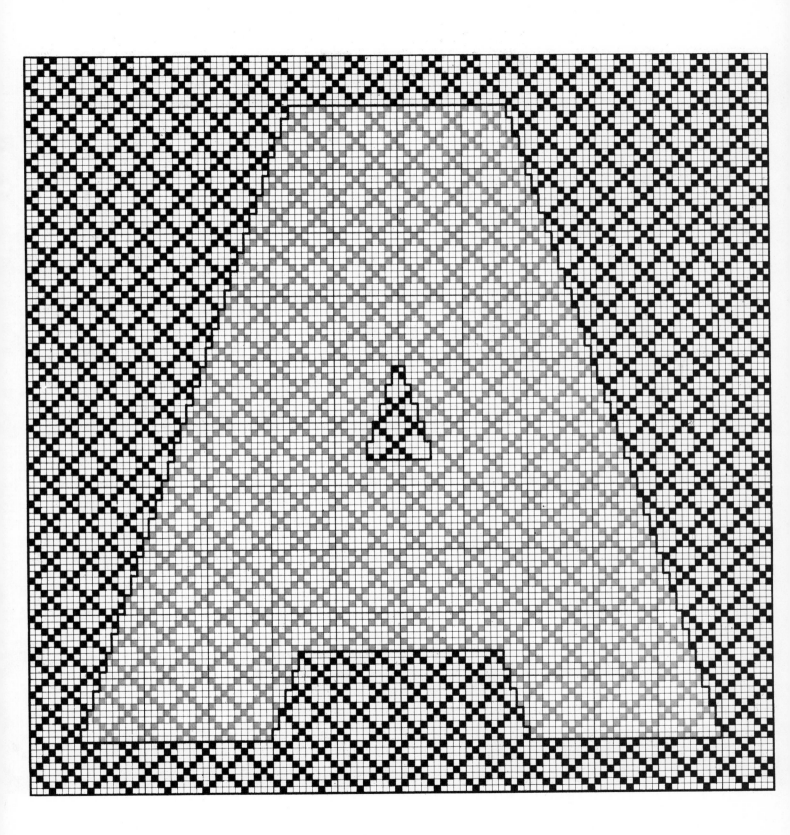

We have shown five borders to be used with the alphabet. You can choose one of these five border designs that is not the same as the geometric design of the background around the letter. The border pattern in conjunction with the pattern of the letter background makes for a very snappy look, giving you pattern on pattern. If you feel this becomes too busy for your personal taste, omit the geometric background around the letter and use only a border pattern. If you choose to use a plain instead of geometric background behind the letter and a border around it, be sure to cut the canvas a total of 4 inches larger horizontally and vertically.

The corners are not a mirror-image. To start the border, begin stitching the lower right hand corner and continue the geometric all around. When the design meets at the beginning, it will match.

In the alphabet section of the book you will see that the five backgrounds we have shown are geometric and must be counted, that is, stitched exactly as shown in the graph. Whichever background you choose, and you may interchange them, start working the upper right-hand corner after you have completed the center design. Once started, it is a simple matter to get it all to come out right.

To determine the correct place to start the geometric pattern for the background when there is an enclosed area in the design, for example a "B" or "R," put a piece of tracing paper over the letter pattern. Clip it to the page so it won't slip. Draw a line across the top and down the right side of the outline border. Trace the opening in the design. Clip this tracing to the geometric design making sure the top vertical and right horizontal lines are squared with the pattern. You will then see where the geometric should be stitched.

8
Rugs and Hangings

These wonderful over-sized canvases can be used for wooly rugs beside a bed, hangings in children's rooms, or backed and stuffed for "poufs," large pillows to sit on. They last better when used for rugs and poufs if they are backed by sailcloth or even a durable gingham. They make wonderful gifts for a host and hostess with children.

Although they are large, stitching them takes an amazingly short time, especially as the canvas is worked and softened.

LETTUCE

Cut a #5 canvas 44 inches by 44 inches, which will include a border for blocking. There will be 189 stitches vertically and 199 stitches horizontally.
The following colors were used (approximate amounts shown in parentheses):

☐	PALE GREEN	P 589	(190 yards)
▦	MEDIUM GREEN	P 579	(202 yards)
■	DARK GREEN	P 559	(90 yards)

THESE 10 SQUARES ARE REPEATED

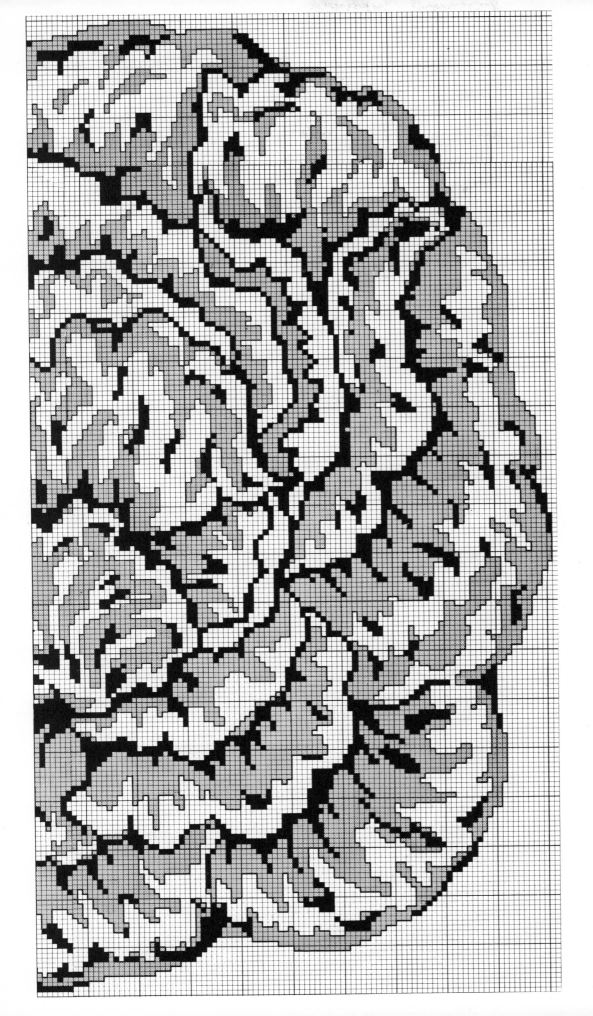

PANSY

Cut a #5 canvas 44 inches by 45 inches including a border for blocking. The stitched area will be 180 by 198.

The following colors were used (approximate amounts shown in parentheses):

☐	LEMON YELLOW	P 483	(167 yards)
E	MUSTARD YELLOW	P 441	(184 yards)
X	ORANGE-RED	P 958	(47 yards)
D	LILAC	P 672	(78 yards)
C	PURPLE	P 622	(77 yards)
B	WHITE	P 010	(4½ yards)
■	TURQUOISE	P 748	(2 yards)
A	MEDIUM GREEN	P 579	(1 yard)

146

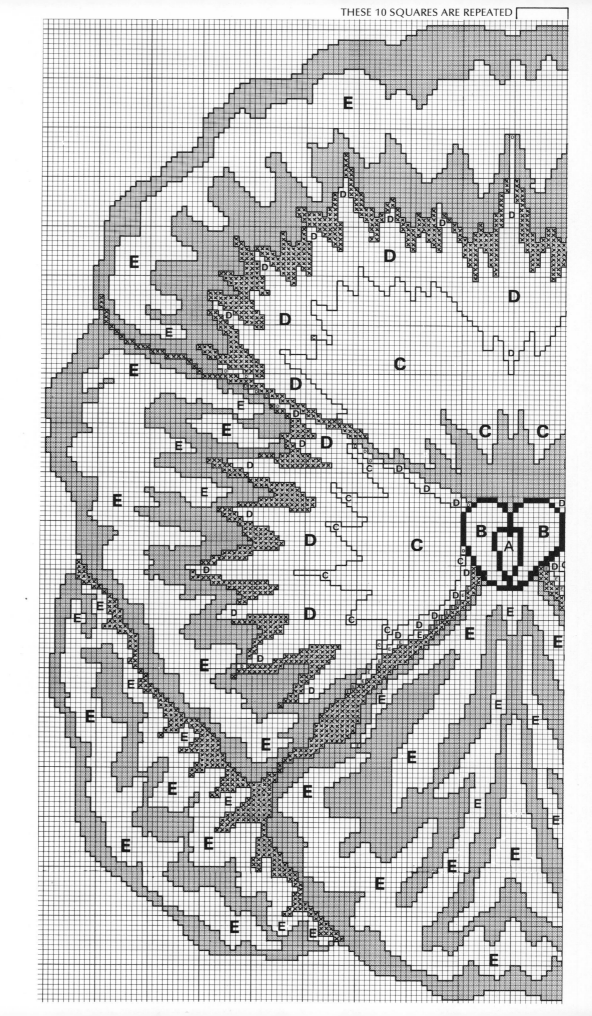

WATERMELON

Cut a #5 canvas 43 inches by 68 inches, which leaves a 4-inch border all around for blocking and hemming. The stitched area, when completed, will measure 34½ inches maximum width by 60 inches maximum length.

The following colors were used (approximate amounts shown in parentheses):

⊡	DARK GREEN	P 559	(113 yards)
Ⓐ	MEDIUM GREEN	P 579	(107 yards)
Ⓑ	WHITE	P 010	(55 yards)
Ⓒ	PALE PINK	P 279	(197 yards)
Ⓓ	MEDIUM PINK	P 259	(175 yards)
⊠	DARK PINK	P 209	(238 yards)
■	BLACK	P 050	(77 yards)

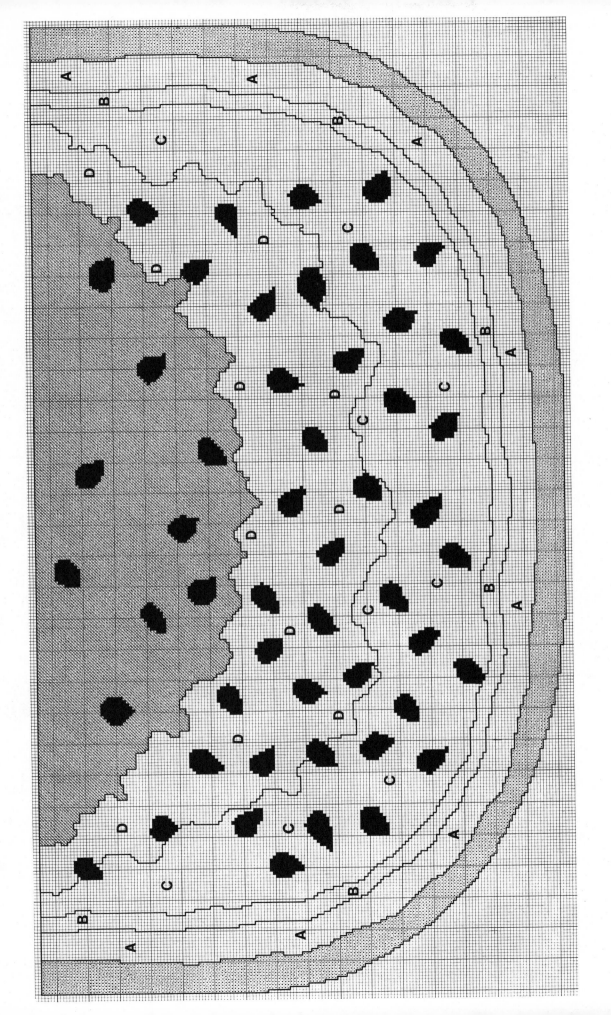

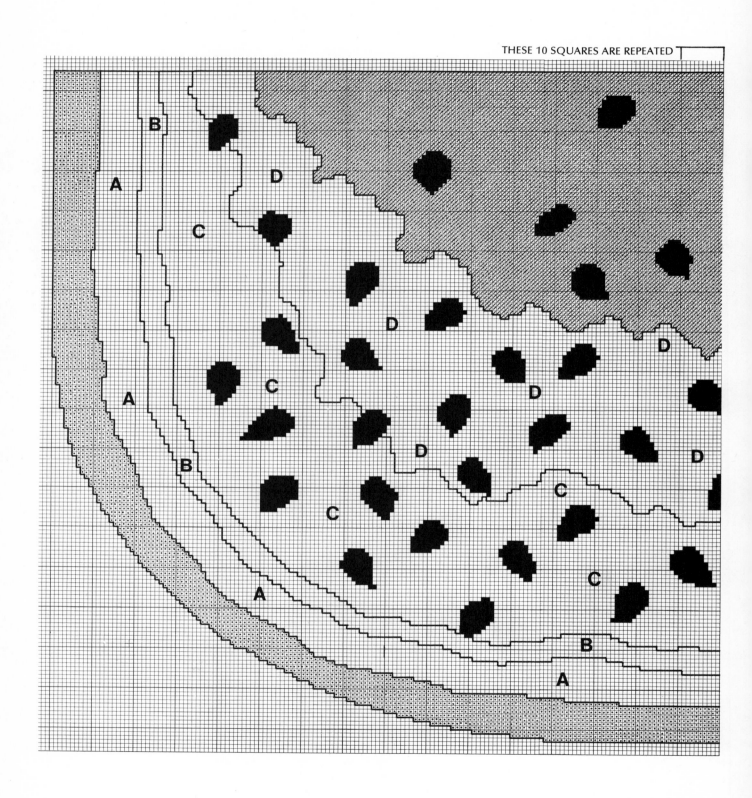

THESE 10 SQUARES ARE REPEATED

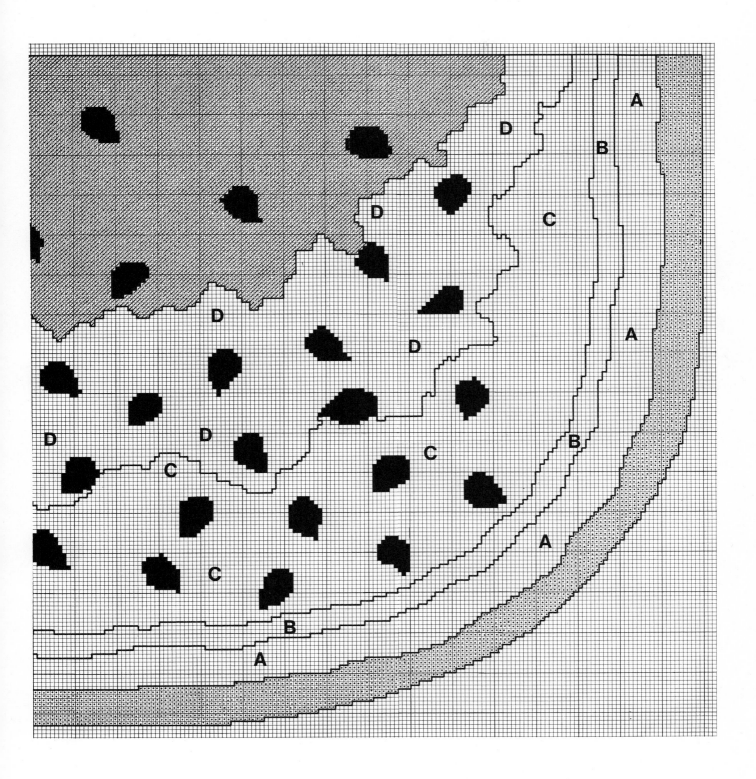

Sources for Needlepoint Supplies

If you cannot find a shop near you that carries supplies we have mentioned, write to any of the following companies enclosing a stamped, self-addressed envelope. They will either give you the address of a retailer in your area or tell you how to order direct.

WOOL, SILK AND COTTON YARNS

Paternayan Brothers
312 East 95th Street
New York, NY 10028

Columbia-Minerva
295 Fifth Avenue
New York, NY 10016

DMC
107 Trumbull Street
Elizabeth, NJ 07206

Craft Yarns of Rhode Island, Inc.
Harrisville, RI 02830

Yarn Loft Imports
P.O. Box 771
Del Mar, CA 92014

CANVAS

Paternayan Brothers
312 East 95th Street
New York, NY 10028

Howard Needlework Supply
919 Third Avenue
New York, NY 10022

C. R. Meissner & Co.
22 East 29th Street
New York, NY 10016
(Meissner will fill mail orders for more than one yard.)

STITCH & ZIP PILLOWS

Alice Peterson
207 Franklin Avenue
El Segundo, CA 90245

TRAYS, TABLES, BOXES, CAMP STOOLS, FOOTSTOOLS

Sudberry House
Box 421
Old Lyme, CT 06371

YARN COLOR ORGANIZER

C. J. Bates & Son
Chester, CT 06412

TAPESTRY CALCULATOR AND STITCH PIC

Needlepoint Technology Co.
P.O. Box 11
Towaco, NJ 07082

NEEDLEPOINT MARKERS

Eberhard Faber
Crestwood
Wilkes-Barre, PA 18703

STITCH CLEAN

Van Wyck Products Co.
Dept. S.B.
120 S. Euclid Avenue
Pasadena, CA 91101

NEEDLEGRAPH

Needlegraph
P.O. Box 186
Dix Hills
Huntington Station, NY 11746

Graph paper can be ordered from Needlegraph in sizes 4, 10, 12, 14, 16 and 18 squares to the inch. The page sizes are 8½" × 11". To make larger sheets, just tape the necessary number of pages together. The paper comes in a 20-sheet package. A minimum of three packages must be ordered; however, all three do not have to be the same graph size.

NEEDLEPOINT BOOKS

Ireys, Katharine, *Finishing and Mounting Your Needlepoint Pieces*. New York: T. Y. Crowell, 1973.

Rome, Carol Cheney, and Donna Reedy Orr, *Needlepoint Letters and Numbers*. New York: Doubleday and Co., 1977.

Bibliography

FOR DESIGN IDEAS

Chwast, Seymour, and Emily Blair Chewning, *The Illustrated Flower*. New York: Harmony Books, 1977.

Faust, Joan Lee, *The New York Times Book of House Plants*. New York: Quadrangle Books, 1973.

Garden Flowers Coloring Book. New York: Dover Publications, Inc., 1975.

Gardening Yearbook. New York: Time-Life Books, Inc., 1978.

Grounds, Roger, and George Elbert, *The 2 Hour Garden*. New York: Doubleday and Co., 1976.

Hersey, Jean, *The Woman's Day Book of Annuals and Perennials*. New York: Simon and Schuster, 1977.

————, *The Woman's Day Book of House Plants*. New York: Simon and Schuster, 1965.

————, *The Woman's Day Book of Wildflowers*. New York: Simon and Schuster, 1976.

Holden, Edith, *The Country Diary of an Edwardian Lady*. New York: Holt, Rinehart and Winston, 1977.

Pizzetti, Ippolito, and Henry Cocker, *A Guide for Your Garden* (2 vols.). New York: Harry N. Abrams, Inc., 1975.

Riker, Tom, and Harvey Rottenberg, *The Gardener's Catalogue*. New York: William Morrow, 1974.

FOR GENERAL GARDENING INFORMATION

Bush-Brown, James and Louise, *America's Garden Book*. New York: Charles Scribner's Sons, 1939.

Crockett, James Underwood, *Crockett's Victory Garden*. Boston: Little, Brown and Co., 1977.

Hay, Roy, and Patrick M. Synge, *The Dictionary of Garden Plants*. London: The Royal Horticultural Society, 1975.

Mossman, Tam, *Gardens That Care for Themselves*. New York: Doubleday and Co., 1978.

Wilson, Helen Van Pelt, *Houseplants Are for Pleasure*. New York: Doubleday and Co., 1973.

About the Authors

JACK BODI, who with his partner, Joseph Leombruno, is a leading photographer, became interested in needlepoint while on an assignment. Unable to find enough good commercial designs, he began to create his own. While working for *Vogue, Glamour,* and *House & Garden,* as well as photographing with Mr. Leombruno for leading advertisers, Mr. Bodi continued to design and stitch his own patterns.

After moving to Italy—where he and Leombruno photographed personalities, fashion, and interiors—Mr. Bodi began to see everyday things in terms of needlecraft, and started the designs for this book. *A Gardener's Book of Needlepoint* is Jack Bodi's garden.

MEG MERRILL came to her first needlepoint book naturally. *Nature in Needlepoint* was an outgrowth of a lifelong concern with nature, conservation, and animal welfare. She is a fashion stylist and skilled needlepointer, and thus *A Gardener's Book of Needlepoint* combines two of her foremost interests. Before beginning her books on needlepoint, Ms. Merrill published several books on small exotic cats, and she still works continuously for animal rights.

Ms. Merrill and her husband, Si, have been nature enthusiasts and avid gardeners during the twenty-four years of their marriage. When they are not traveling extensively, they live in New York City and on Long Island with their son, Michael, and, until recently, a South American margay cat that they rescued from a pet dealer.

CATHERINE DI MONTEZEMOLO was on the fashion editorial staff of *Vogue* for twenty-five years, until 1973, when her husband was transferred to Milan, Italy, where they lived for two years. During that time she became European editor of *Harper's Bazaar.* On her return to the United States she began her own business, designing sleepwear and at-home clothes labeled "Cathy di Montezemolo." She is now also a contributing editor of *House & Garden.*